SECOND EDITION

TOUCHSTONE

STUDENT'S BOOK 1B

MICHAEL MCCARTHY
JEANNE MCCARTEN
HELEN SANDIFORD

CAMBRIDGE
UNIVERSITY PRESS

CAMBRIDGE
UNIVERSITY PRESS & ASSESSMENT

Shaftesbury Road, Cambridge CB2 8EA, United Kingdom

One Liberty Plaza, 20th Floor, New York, NY 10006, USA

477 Williamstown Road, Port Melbourne, VIC 3207, Australia

314–321, 3rd Floor, Plot 3, Splendor Forum, Jasola District Centre, New Delhi – 110025, India

103 Penang Road, #05-06/07, Visioncrest Commercial, Singapore 238467

Cambridge University Press & Assessment is a department of the University of Cambridge.

We share the University's mission to contribute to society through the pursuit of education, learning and research at the highest international levels of excellence.

www.cambridge.org
Information on this title: www.cambridge.org/9781107653450

First published 2005
Second Edition 2014

20 19 18 17

Printed in Mexico by Litográfica Ingramex, S.A. de C.V.

A catalogue record for this publication is available from the British Library

ISBN 978-1-107-67987-0 Student's Book
ISBN 978-1-107-62792-5 Student's Book A
ISBN 978-1-107-65345-0 Student's Book B
ISBN 978-1-107-63933-1 Workbook
ISBN 978-1-107-67071-6 Workbook A
ISBN 978-1-107-69125-4 Workbook B
ISBN 978-1-107-68330-3 Full Contact
ISBN 978-1-107-66769-3 Full Contact A
ISBN 978-1-107-61366-9 Full Contact B
ISBN 978-1-107-64223-2 Teacher's Edition with Assessment Audio CD/CD-ROM
ISBN 978-1-107-61414-7 Class Audio CDs (4)

Additional resources for this publication at www.cambridge.org/touchstone2

Acknowledgments

Touchstone Second Edition **has benefited from extensive development research. The authors and publishers would like to extend their thanks to the following reviewers and consultants for their valuable insights and suggestions:**

Ana Lúcia da Costa Maia de Almeida and Mônica da Costa Monteiro de Souza from **IBEU**, Rio de Janeiro, Brazil; Andreza Cristiane Melo do Lago from **Magic English School,** Manaus, Brazil; Magaly Mendes Lemos from **ICBEU**, São José dos Campos, Brazil; Maria Lucia Zaorob, São Paulo, Brazil; Patricia McKay Aronis from **CEL LEP**, São Paulo, Brazil; Carlos Gontow, São Paulo, Brazil; Christiane Augusto Gomes da Silva from **Colégio Visconde de Porto Seguro,** São Paulo, Brazil; Silvana Fontana from **Lord's Idiomas**, São Paulo, Brazil; Alexander Fabiano Morishigue from **Speed Up Idiomas**, Jales, Brazil; Elisabeth Blom from **Casa Thomas Jefferson**, Brasília, Brazil; Michelle Dear from **International Academy of English**, Toronto, ON, Canada; Walter Duarte Marin, Laura Hurtado Portela, Jorge Quiroga, and Ricardo Suarez, from **Centro Colombo Americano**, Bogotá, Colombia; Jhon Jairo Castaneda Macias from **Praxis English Academy**, Bucaramanga, Colombia; Gloria Liliana Moreno Vizcaino from **Universidad Santo Tomas**, Bogotá, Colombia; Elizabeth Ortiz from **Copol English Institute (COPEI),** Guayaquil, Ecuador; Henry Foster from **Kyoto Tachibana University,** Kyoto, Japan; Steven Kirk from **Tokyo University**, Tokyo, Japan; J. Lake from **Fukuoka Woman's University**, Fukuoka, Japan; Etsuko Yoshida from **Mie University**, Mie, Japan; B. Bricklin Zeff from **Hokkai Gakuen University**, Hokkaido, Japan; Ziad Abu-Hamatteh from **Al-Balqa' Applied University**, Al-Salt, Jordan; Roxana Pérez Flores from **Universidad Autonoma de Coahuila Language Center**, Saltillo, Mexico; Kim Alejandro Soriano Jimenez from **Universidad Politecnica de Altamira**, Altamira, Mexico; Tere Calderon Rosas from **Universidad Autonoma Metropolitana Campus Iztapalapa**, Mexico City, Mexico; Lilia Bondareva, Polina Ermakova, and Elena Frumina, from **National Research Technical University MISiS**, Moscow, Russia; Dianne C. Ellis from **Kyung Hee University**, Gyeonggi-do, South Korea; Jason M. Ham and Victoria Jo from **Institute of Foreign Language Education, Catholic University of Korea**, Gyeonggi-do, South Korea; Shaun Manning from **Hankuk University of Foreign Studies**, Seoul, South Korea; Natalie Renton from **Busan National University of Education**, Busan, South Korea; Chris Soutter from **Busan University of Foreign Studies**, Busan, South Korea; Andrew Cook from **Dong A University**, Busan, South Korea; Raymond Wowk from **Daejin University**, Gyeonggi-do, South Korea; Ming-Hui Hsieh and Jessie Huang from **National Central University**, Zhongli, Taiwan; Kim Phillips from **Chinese Culture University**, Taipei, Taiwan; Alex Shih from **China University of Technology**, Taipei Ta-Liao Township, Taiwan; Porntip Bodeepongse from **Thaksin University**, Songkhla, Thailand; Nattaya Puakpong and Pannathon Sangarun from **Suranaree University of Technology**, Nakhon Ratchasima, Thailand; Barbara Richards, Gloria Stewner-Manzanares, and Caroline Thompson, from **Montgomery College**, Rockville, MD, USA; Kerry Vrabel from **Gateway Community College**, Phoenix, AZ, USA.

Touchstone Second Edition **authors and publishers would also like to thank the following individuals and institutions who have provided excellent feedback and support on** ***Touchstone Blended:***

Gordon Lewis, Vice President, Laureate Languages and Chris Johnson, Director, Laureate English Programs, Latin America from **Laureate International Universities**; **Universidad de las Americas**, Santiago, Chile; **University of Victoria**, Paris, France; **Universidad Technólogica Centroamericana**, Honduras; **Instititut Universitaire de Casablanca**, Morocco; **Universidad Peruana de Ciencias Aplicadas**, Lima, Peru; **CIBERTEC**, Peru; **National Research Technical University (MiSIS)**, Moscow, Russia; **Institut Obert de Catalunya (IOC),** Barcelona, Spain; Sedat Çilingir, Burcu Tezcan, and Didem Mutçalıoğlu from **İstanbul Bilgi Üniversitesi,** Istanbul, Turkey.

Touchstone Second Edition **authors and publishers would also like to thank the following contributors to** ***Touchstone Second Edition:***

Sue Aldcorn, Frances Amrani, Deborah Gordon, Lisa Hutchins, Nancy Jordan, Steven Kirk, Genevieve Kocienda, Linda-Marie Koza, Geraldine Mark, Julianna Nielsen, Kathryn O'Dell, Nicola Prentis, Ellen Shaw, Kristin Sherman, Luis Silva Susa, Mary Vaughn, Kerry S. Vrabel, Shari Young and Eric Zuarino.

Authors' Acknowledgments

The authors would like to thank all the Cambridge University Press staff and freelancers who were involved in the creation of *Touchstone Second Edition*. In addition, they would like to acknowledge a huge debt of gratitude that they owe to two people: Mary Vaughn, for her role in creating *Touchstone First Edition* and for being a constant source of wisdom ever since, and Bryan Fletcher, who also had the vision that has led to the success of *Touchstone Blended Learning*.

Helen Sandiford would like to thank her family for their love and support, especially her husband Bryan.

The author team would also like to thank each other, for the joy of working together, sharing the same professional dedication, and for the mutual support and friendship.

Finally, the authors would like to thank our dear friend Alejandro Martinez, Global Training Manager, who sadly passed away in 2012. He is greatly missed by all who had the pleasure to work with him. Alex was a huge supporter of *Touchstone* and everyone is deeply grateful to him for his contribution to its success.

Touchstone Level 1B Contents and learning outcomes

Interaction	Skills				Self study
Conversation strategies	**Listening**	**Reading**	**Writing**	**Free talk**	**Vocabulary notebook**
• Ask follow-up questions to keep a conversation going • React with expressions like *That's great!* and *That's too bad*	***That's great!*** • Listen to people tell you their news and choose a good follow-up question to ask them ***Do you enjoy it?*** • Listen to people talk about exercises they like	***Exergaming: Give it a try!*** • Read an article about exergaming	***An article for a health magazine*** • Write a short article giving advice about exercise • Use imperatives to give advice	***Find out about your classmates*** • Class activity: Learn interesting facts about classmates	***Who's doing what?*** • Write new words in true sentences
• Take time to think using *Uh, Um, Well, Let's see,* and *Let me think* • Use "sounds" like *Uh-huh* to show you are listening, and *Oh* to show your feelings	***I'll take it.*** • Listen to conversations in a store, and write the prices of items and which items people buy ***Favorite places to shop*** • Listen to someone talk about shopping, and identify shopping preferences and habits	***The Dubai Mall: Shopping, Entertainment, Lifestyle*** • Read a review of a mall	***Favorite places to shop*** • Write a review for your favorite store • Link ideas with *because* to give reasons	***How do you like to dress?*** • Group work: Compare ideas about shopping and clothing	***Nice outfit!*** • Label pictures with new vocabulary
• Explain words using *a kind of, kind of like,* and *like* • Use *like* to give examples	***International dishes*** • Listen to a person talking about international foods, and identify the foods she likes ***What language is it from?*** • Listen to a conversation, and identify the origin and meaning of words	***The Travel Guide*** • Read a travel website	***An online travel guide*** • Write a paragraph for a travel guide • Commas in lists	***Where in the world?*** • Pair work: Discuss where to do various things in the world	***People and nations*** • Group new vocabulary in two ways
Checkpoint Units 7–9 pages 95–96					
• Respond with expressions like *Good luck, You poor thing*, etc. • Use *You did?* to show that you are interested or surprised, or that you are listening	***Good week? Bad week?*** • Listen to people talk about their week and respond ***Guess what I did!*** • Listen to voice mail messages about what people did	***She said yes!!!*** • Read Martin's Blog entry	***A great day*** • Write a blog entry • Order events with *before, after, when,* and *then*	***Yesterday*** • Pair work: Look at a picture and list what you remember	***Ways with verbs*** • Write down information about new verbs
• Show interest by answering a question and then asking a similar one • Use *Anyway* to change the topic or end a conversation	***Weekend fun*** • Listen to conversations about peoples' weekends, and identify main topics and details ***Funny stories*** • Listen to two stories, identify the details, and then predict the endings	***How embarrassing!*** • Read a funny magazine story	***He said, she said*** • Complete a funny story • Use punctuation to show direct quotations or speech	***Guess where I went on vacation.*** • Group work: Guess classmates' dream vacations	***Past experiences*** • Use a time chart to log new vocabulary
• Use *or something* and *or anything* to make a general statement • End *yes-no* questions with *or . . . ?* to be less direct	***If you want my advice . . .*** • Listen to people talking about lunch, and identify what they want; then react to statements ***Do you recommend it?*** • Listen to someone tell a friend about a restaurant and identify important details about it	***Restaurant guide*** • Restaurant descriptions and recommendations	***Do you recommend it?*** • Write a restaurant review • Use adjectives to describe restaurants	***Plan a picnic*** • Group work: Plan a picnic menu and make a shopping list	***I love to eat!*** • Group vocabulary by things you like and don't like
Checkpoint Units 10–12 pages 127–128					

Useful language for . . .

Getting help

What's the word for "________" in English?

How do you spell "________"?

What does "________" mean?

I'm sorry. Can you repeat that, please?

Can you say that again, please?

Can you explain the activity again, please?

Working with a partner

I'm ready. Are you ready?

No. Just a minute.

You go first.

OK. I'll go first.

What do you have for number 1?

I have . . .

Do you want to be A or B?

I'll be A. You can be B.

Let's do the activity again.

OK. Let's change roles.

That's it. We're finished.

What do we do next?

Can I read your paragraph?

Sure. Here you go.

UNIT 7

Out and about

Can Do! In this unit, you learn how to . . .

Lesson A
- Describe the weather
- Talk about ongoing activities with the present continuous

Lesson B
- Talk about sports and exercise
- Ask about current activities using the present continuous

Lesson C
- Ask follow-up questions to keep a conversation going
- React to news with *That's great, That's too bad*, etc.

Lesson D
- Read an article about exergaming
- Write an article about exercise using imperatives

1

2

3

4

5

6

Before you begin . . .

Match the pictures and seasons. Which seasons do you have? What's the weather usually like in each season?

☐ spring
1 summer
☐ fall
☐ winter
☐ rainy season
☐ dry season

It's hot and humid.
It's warm and sunny.
It's cool. It's often cloudy.
It's windy. It's cold.
It rains.
It snows.

Lesson A / Away for the weekend

It's 2:30 p.m. on Saturday, and Anita is at work in San Francisco. She usually relaxes on Saturdays, but she's working this weekend. Right now she's taking a break and listening to her voice mail. All her friends are having fun!

Saturday, 8:45 a.m.
Hi, Anita. This is Yoko. I'm calling from a ski resort in Lake Tahoe. Lisa and I are skiing today. It's so beautiful here, and there's lots of snow. It's snowing right now. I'm sorry you're working. What's the weather like in San Francisco? Give me a call. Bye.

Saturday, 10:20 a.m.
Hi, it's Bill. Listen, Marcos and I are at the beach in Santa Cruz. Come and join us! Don't worry – we're not swimming. It's too cold and cloudy. See you.

Saturday, 11:15 a.m.
Hey, Anita. This is Nathan. I'm in San Jose with Katie and Rob. They're playing tennis, and I'm watching. It's nice and sunny. I hope it's not raining there. Call me! Bye.

1 Getting started

A **Look at the pictures. Where is Anita? Where are her friends?**

B 2.24 **Listen. What's the weather like in each place?**

Figure it out **C** **What are Anita and her friends doing? Circle the correct words.**

1. Anita usually relaxes on Saturdays, but today **she works / she's working**!
2. Yoko says, "Lisa and I **am / are** skiing today. **It snows / It's snowing** here right now."
3. Bill says, "Marcos and I are at the beach . . . **we're not / we don't** swimming. It's too cold!"
4. Nathan says, "I'm in San Jose with Katie and Rob. **They / They're** playing tennis."

2 Grammar Present continuous statements 2.25

Extra practice p. 145

Use the present continuous to talk about right now or today.

I'm	(not)	**calling**	from home.
You'**re**		**working**	today.
She'**s**		**skiing**	with a friend.
He'**s**		**having**	fun.
It'**s**		**raining**	right now.
We'**re**		**swimming**	in the ocean.
They'**re**		**playing**	tennis.

The contractions *isn't* and *aren't* often follow nouns:

Marcos **isn't** working.
Marcos and Bill **aren't** swimming.

Spelling

work ▶ work**ing**
swim ▶ swim**ming**
have ▶ hav**ing**

In conversation

In the present continuous, people usually use *'s not* and *'re not* after pronouns. People don't usually say *we aren't, they aren't, he isn't,* etc.

A 2.26 **Complete Anita's other voice mail messages. Then listen and check.**

1
Saturday, 11:45 a.m.
Hi, Anita. This is Andrea. I'm calling (call) from the mall. I'm in a café with Chris. We ______ (have) lunch right now. Chris ______ (not stay) long. He ______ (shop) for a new computer. So let's meet. Give me a call. See you!

2
Saturday, 1:30 p.m.
Hey, Anita, it's me, John. I'm at Andrew's house. We ______ (watch) the baseball game. The Giants ______ (not play) very well. And now it ______ (rain). Um, let's meet for dinner. Call me on my cell. Bye.

3
Saturday, 2:00 p.m.
Hi. Where are you? I hope you ______ (not work). Listen, Chloe ______ (not work) today, and I ______ (not do) anything special. You know, I ______ (clean) the house, and Chloe ______ (do) laundry. So come over around 5:00, and have an early dinner. Call me.

B **Prepare a voice mail message for a friend. Then take turns saying your messages to the class. Who's having the most fun?**

"Hi there. This is ______.
I'm at ______.
I'm ______.
The weather is ______ it ______."

Common errors

Always use *be* with the present continuous.

It's raining. (NOT ~~*It raining*~~.)

3 Talk about it What's your "perfect" day?

A **Imagine you are having a perfect day. Think of answers to the questions below.**

- Where are you?
- What's the weather like?
- Who are you with?
- What are you doing?

"On my perfect day, I'm at the beach. It's very hot and I'm sleeping. I'm . . ."

About you **B** **Class activity** Go around the class, and tell your classmates about your perfect day. Can you find anyone with the same ideas?

Sports and exercise

1 Building vocabulary

A 2.27 Listen and repeat the sentences.

They're playing . . .

They're doing . . .

They're . . .

Word sort **B** Complete the chart with the activities above and add your own ideas. Compare with a partner.

I often . . .	Sometimes I . . .	I never . . .
go running.	*do aerobics.*	*play soccer.*

Note

I'm **bowling / running / biking** right now.
I **go bowling / running / biking** every week.

Vocabulary notebook p. 74

2 Building language

A 2.28 Listen. Is Carl studying hard this semester? What is he doing right now? Practice the conversation.

Dad Hi, Carl. It's me. How's it going?
Carl Oh, hi, Dad. Everything's great.
Dad So are you studying for your exams?
Carl Oh, yeah. I'm working very hard this semester.
Dad Good. So what are you doing right now? Are you studying?
Carl Uh, Dad, right now I'm watching a baseball game.
Dad Baseball? . . . Uh, who's playing?
Carl The Yankees and the Red Sox.
Dad Really? Uh, Carl, . . . let's talk again in two hours.
Carl OK, Dad. Enjoy the game!
Dad You too. But please try and study for your exams!

Figure it out **B** Underline the questions in the conversation above. What do you notice about the word order?

3 Grammar Present continuous questions 2.29

Extra practice p. 145

Information questions

What **are** you **doing** these days?
What **is** Carl **watching** on TV?
Who **'s** he **talking** to right now?

Information questions with *who* as subject

Who **'s playing?** (The Yankees.)
Who **'s watching** the game? (Carl.)

***Yes-no* questions and short answers**

Are	you	**studying** hard?	Yes, I **am.**	No, I'**m not.**
Is	Carl	**watching** the game?	Yes, he **is.**	No, he'**s not.**
Are	the Yankees	**playing?**	Yes, they **are.**	No, they'**re not.**

You can use the present continuous for activities "around now."
I'm working very hard this semester.

Time expressions
right now
today
this morning
this week
this month
this year
this semester
this season
these days

A Complete the questions with the present continuous.

1. What *are* you *doing* (do) for exercise these days?
2. ________ you ________ (run)? ________ you ________ (swim)?
3. ________ you ________ (get) enough exercise?
4. ________ your best friend ________ (take) an exercise class?
5. Who ________ ________ (exercise) more – you or your best friend?
6. ________ you ________ (watch) any special sporting events on TV this week?
7. ________ your friends ________ (play) on any sports teams this year? How about you?
8. How ________ your favorite sports team ________ (do) this season? Who on the team ________ ________ (play) well?

About you **B Pair work** Ask and answer the questions. Give your own answers.

A ***What are you doing for exercise these days?***
B ***Well, I'm taking a weights class at the gym this month.***

4 Speaking naturally Stress and intonation in questions

*How often do you go to the **gym**?* *Are you going a **lot** these days?*

A 2.30 Listen and repeat the questions. Notice how the words *gym* and *lot* are stressed. Notice how the voice falls on *gym* and rises on *lot.*

B 2.31 Listen. Repeat these pairs of questions.

1. How often do you play **sports**? Are you playing a **lot** these days?
2. When do you **study**? Are you studying **hard** right now?
3. How are your **classes** going this year? I mean, are they going **well**?

About you **C Pair work** Ask and answer the questions above. Give your own answers.

Sounds right p. 138

How's it going?

1 Conversation strategy Asking follow-up questions

A Look at the picture of Tina, Kate, and Ray. What are they doing?

B 2.32 Listen. What is Kate doing in Laguna Beach this week?

Tina	Hey, Ray, this is my friend Kate. She's visiting from Chicago.
Ray	Oh, hi. Nice to meet you. So, uh . . . are you here on vacation?
Kate	Yeah, I'm here for a week.
Ray	That's great! Are you enjoying Laguna Beach?
Kate	Yeah! I'm taking a scuba-diving course.
Ray	That's cool. How's it going?
Kate	Really well. And I'm having a great time.
Tina	Oh, that's my cell phone. Excuse me.
Ray	Sure.

C Notice how Ray asks Kate questions. He keeps the conversation going. Find examples in the conversation.

"I'm here for a week."
"That's great! Are you enjoying Laguna Beach?"

D 2.33 Complete the conversations with the follow-up questions. There is one extra question. Then listen and check your answers. Practice with a partner.

1. A You know, I'm taking a French class.
   B Really? ____________________
   A Yeah. It's going pretty well. I like it.
   B That's good. ____________________
   A Yeah. It's interesting. So how about you? ____________________

2. A I'm reading a couple of really good books.
   B Yeah? ____________________
   A Oh, a book by Suzanne Collins, and a book about music.
   B That's interesting. ____________________

- Are you taking any interesting classes?
- Are you enjoying it?
- So do you have an e-reader?
- Are you learning about the culture, too?
- So where are you going? To clubs?
- What are you reading?

2 Strategy plus *That's . . .*

You can use expressions with *That's . . .* to react to news.

In conversation

The top expressions for good news are:

*That's **good** / **great** / **nice** / **interesting** / **cool** / **wonderful**.*

The top expressions for bad news are:

*Oh, that's **too bad** / **terrible**.*

Complete the responses using an expression with *That's*. Then practice with a partner.

1. A I'm taking a yoga course this week. I'm really enjoying it.
   B Oh, ______________________ .
2. A I'm feeling really tired. I'm not sleeping well and I'm not eating.
   B Really? ______________________ .
3. A A friend of mine is studying sports science.
   B Really? ______________________ .
4. A My friends are on vacation this week. They're biking in the Alps.
   B Oh, ______________________ .

3 Listening and strategies That's great!

A 2.34 **Listen to six people tell you their news. Respond using an expression with *That's*. Then choose a good follow-up question. Write the letters *a* to *f*.**

1. That's __________ . _____
2. That's __________ . _____
3. That's __________ . _____
4. That's __________ . _____
5. That's __________ . _____
6. That's __________ . _____

a. So what are you reading right now?
b. Who's playing?
c. So what are you doing? I mean, are you making coffee?
d. It sounds interesting. Is it playing every day?
e. What's she doing all day? Is she blogging?
f. Why is he seeing her? Do you know?

B 2.34 **Listen again. Write one piece of information about each person's news.**

About you **C Pair work** **Take turns telling your partner some interesting news. Respond with *That's . . .* and ask follow-up questions.**

A I'm playing on the school volleyball team this year.
B That's great. How's the team doing?

Free talk p. 133

1 Reading

A For which exercise activities do you do these things? Tell the class.

- have a personal trainer
- pay a fee
- buy special equipment
- get feedback on your progress

Reading tip

Read the main headings first. They tell you what the article covers.

B Read the article. Why is exergaming a good idea?

EXERGAMING *Give it a try!*

College student Aaron Case plays tennis every day, even when it's raining – like today. But Aaron isn't getting wet. He's playing against a virtual tennis professional on his TV. These days, there are millions of "exergamers" like Aaron. They're skiing, playing golf, and doing karate in their own homes. Video exercise games are popular with people of all ages, and it's easy to see why.

- ▶ **The weather is never a problem.** Is it raining or snowing? Maybe it's hot and humid outside. Don't worry. Exercise indoors.
- ▶ **It's convenient.** Stay home and work out in front of your TV!
- ▶ **It's motivating.** Don't pay for an expensive personal trainer. With exergaming, you see your scores and get feedback on your progress.
- ▶ **There's variety.** Try something new. Exergames have everything from aerobics to yoga. There are a lot of different types of games, so you never get bored.
- ▶ **It's fun.** Work out with a friend, or play a game with a family member.
- ▶ **It's not expensive.** Forget about monthly gym fees. Just buy the basic equipment and a game, and after that, exergaming is free!

So, if you're looking for convenient, cheap, and fun ways to exercise, why not give exergaming a try?

C According to the article, are these sentences true or false? Check (✓) *True* (T) or *False* (F). Correct the false statements.

	T	F
1. Aaron Case is playing tennis outdoors in the rain.	☐	☐
2. Only young people enjoy exergaming.	☐	☐
3. Some personal trainers are expensive.	☐	☐
4. Exergamers don't get bored.	☐	☐
5. You pay monthly fees for some games.	☐	☐
6. The equipment for exergaming is free.	☐	☐

About you **D** **Pair work** Do you agree that exergaming is good exercise? Why or why not? Discuss with your partner.

2 Listening Do you enjoy it?

A Look at the pictures below. What are the people doing? Do you or your friends do these things?

B 2.35 Listen to four conversations. Number the pictures 1 to 4.

☐

☐

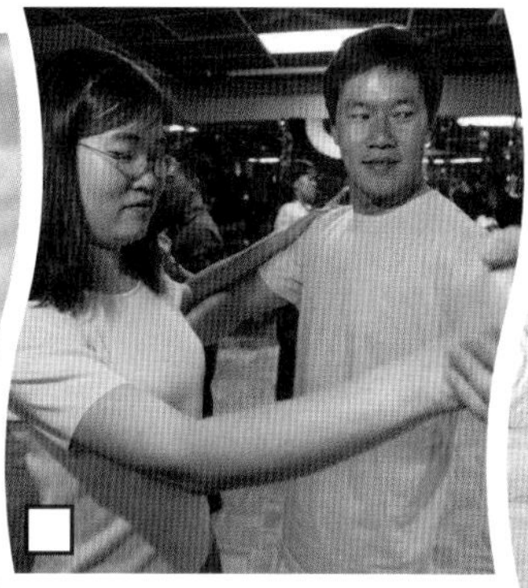
☐

☐

C 2.35 Listen again. Answer the questions in the chart.

	How often do the people do the activities?	What do they like about the activities?
1.		
2.		
3.		
4.		

About you **D** **Pair work** What do you think about the different activities above? Discuss the pros and cons.

3 Writing Get moving!

A Read the Help note and the article. Underline the verbs that are imperatives for advice.

Try aerobics!

Are you exercising enough? A lot of people are taking aerobics classes these days. Why?

1. **Aerobics is fun.**
   Find a fun teacher, and make new friends with your classmates. Don't be shy!
2. **Aerobics is good for you.**
   It's good for your heart, and you feel great after class. Don't miss a class.
3. **Aerobics is easy.**
   Buy an aerobics game and exercise in front of your TV. Do it before breakfast.

Help note

Imperatives for advice

An imperative = verb

- ***Find*** *a fun teacher.*
- ***Make*** *new friends.*

A negative imperative = *Don't* + verb

- ***Don't be*** *shy!*
- ***Don't miss*** *a class.*

About you **B** Choose an exercise activity you enjoy. Write an article giving ideas and advice like the one above.

C **Pair work** Read a classmate's article. Ask questions to find out more information.

Learning tip *Writing true sentences*

To remember new vocabulary, use words in true sentences.

In conversation

It's cold outside!

In the U.S. and Canada, the top six weather expressions with ***it's*** are:

1. It's cold.
2. It's hot.
3. It's raining.
4. It's windy.
5. It's humid.
6. It's snowing.

People say ***It's cold*** 10 times more than ***It's hot***.

1 Complete the sentences about the weather.

1. Right now it ________________ outside.
2. At this time of year, it usually ________________ .
3. In the summer, it ________________ .
4. In the winter, it ________________ .
5. I like the weather when it ________________ ,
   but I don't like it when it ________________ .

2 Write the names of at least three people you know. Complete the chart with true sentences.

	Name	Where is he or she right now?	What is he or she doing right now?	What is he or she doing these days?
1	*my brother Juan*	*He's at school.*	*He's studying math right now.*	*He's playing soccer and basketball.*
2				
3				
4				
5				
6				

On your own

Take a minute this week, and look around you. What are people doing? Write six sentences.

Can Do! Now I can . . .

✓ I can . . . ? I need to review how to . . .

- ☐ describe the weather.
- ☐ talk about sports and exercise.
- ☐ ask questions about what people are doing.
- ☐ keep a conversation going.
- ☐ react to good or bad news.
- ☐ listen and respond to people's news.
- ☐ understand people talking about their exercise routines.
- ☐ read an article about exergaming.
- ☐ write a short article giving advice about exercise.

UNIT 8

Shopping

Can Do! In this unit, you learn how to . . .

Lesson A
- Talk about clothes
- Say what you *like to, want to, need to,* and *have to* do

Lesson B
- Talk about accessories
- Ask about prices using *How much . . . ?, this, that, these,* and *those*

Lesson C
- Take time to think using *Uh, Let's see,* etc.
- Use *Uh-huh* and *Oh* in responses

Lesson D
- Read a review of a shopping mall
- Write a review of a store using *because*

Before you begin . . .

Look at the pictures. What are the people wearing? What are your classmates wearing? Use the words below.

- pants and a top
- a dress and high heels
- jeans
- a cardigan
- a sweatshirt
- a suit and tie
- sweatpants
- a T-shirt

Lesson A Clothes

What kinds of clothes do you like to wear?

Kyoko Takano, 16, high school student

Well, we don't have to wear uniforms at our school, so I like to wear pants, a T-shirt, and sneakers. So yeah, I'm lucky. My friend has to wear a uniform, and she hates it.

Emre Yilmaz, 27, accountant

I have to wear a suit and tie to work. After work, I just want to go home and put on jeans and an old sweater. You know, something comfortable.

Bethany Philips, 32, advertising executive

Well, my boss likes to wear designer clothes, so I need to look good, too. I usually wear a nice skirt or dressy pants with a silk blouse, and a jacket. Oh, and high heels.

1 Getting started

A Look at the photos above. Who is wearing these things?

a jacket ____________ a silk blouse ____________ a skirt ____________
sneakers ____________ a sweater ____________

B 2.36 Listen. Who wears casual clothes to school or work? Who wears formal clothes?

Figure it out **C** Circle the correct words. Use the interviews above to help you.

1. Emre says, "After work, I just **want / want to** put on jeans and an old sweater."
2. Kyoko says, "I like **to wear / wear** pants, a T-shirt, and sneakers."
3. Kyoko doesn't **have / have to** wear a uniform. She doesn't need to **wear / wearing** formal clothes.
4. Bethany's boss wears designer clothes, so Louisa **has to / has** look good, too.

About you **D** **Pair work** Are you like Kyoko, Emre, or Bethany? Tell a partner.

2 Grammar *Like to, want to, need to, have to* 2.37

Extra practice p. 146

After the verbs *want* and *like*, you can use *to* + verb.

What do you **want to wear** tonight?
I **want to wear** my new outfit.
I don't **want to wear** my old dress.

What kinds of clothes does Bethany **like to wear** to work?
She **likes to wear** designer clothes.
She doesn't **like to wear** casual clothes to work.

Use *need to* + verb and *have to* + verb to talk about needs and rules.

What do you **need to buy**?
Do you **need to buy** new shoes?
Yes, I do. I **need to get** some sneakers.

What does Emre **have to wear** to work?
Does he **have to wear** a suit?
Yes, he does. He **has to wear** a suit and tie.

About you **Complete the conversations. Practice with a partner. Then ask the questions again and give your own answers.**

1. A What do you *like to wear* (like / wear) at home in the evening?
   B I usually just ____________ (want / relax). I ____________ (like / put on) jeans.
2. A Do your friends ____________ (have to / wear) a uniform to school or work?
   B No, they don't. My friend Jenna ____________ (have to / look) good for work. But she ____________ (not have to / wear) a uniform.
3. A Do you ____________ (like / buy) clothes online? Or do you ____________ (have to / see) things first?
   B No, I always ____________ (need / try on) clothes. So I ____________ (not like / shop) online.
4. A Are stores expensive here? I mean, do you ____________ (have to / pay) a lot for jeans?
   B Well, there are expensive stores. But you ____________ (not need / shop) at those places.

Common errors

Simple present short answers end with a form of *do*.

Do you like to wear jeans?
No, I ***don't***. (NOT ~~*No, I don't like*~~.)

3 Speaking naturally *Want to* and *have to*

"wanna" *I* ***want to*** *buy some new clothes.*
What do you ***want to*** *buy?*

"hafta" *I* ***have to*** *buy some new clothes.*
What do you ***have to*** *buy?*

A 2.38 **Listen and repeat the sentences above. Notice the reduction of *want to* and *have to*.**

B 2.39 **Now listen and repeat these questions.**

1. Do you have to go shopping this week? . . . Where do you have to go?
2. Do you have to buy any new clothes? . . . What do you have to get?
3. Do you want to spend a lot of money? . . . How much do you want to spend?
4. Do you want to go to a designer store? . . . Which stores do you want to go to?

About you **C Pair work** **Ask and answer the questions above. What do you and your partner have in common?**

A ***Do you have to go shopping this week?***
B ***Yes, I have to go shopping on Saturday.***

1 Building vocabulary

A 2.40 Listen and say the words. Which items do you have? Which do you want to buy? Tell the class.

Word sort **B** 2.41 Listen and say the names of the colors. What clothes and accessories do you have in these colors? Write them in the chart. Compare with a partner.

white	black	red	blue	brown	green	yellow	gray	pink	orange
	jeans								

"I have three pairs of black jeans. I like to wear black."

Vocabulary notebook p. 84

2 Building language

A 2.42 Listen. How much are the gloves and the scarf? Practice the conversation.

Salesperson Hello. Can I help you?
Stacy Uh, hi. How much are those gloves?
Salesperson These? They're really popular. They're $80.
Stacy Hmm. And what about that blue scarf? How much is that?
Salesperson This scarf is on sale. It's only $149.
Stacy A hundred and forty-nine dollars? OK, I have to think about it. Thanks anyway.

Figure it out **B** Circle the correct word in each sentence. Then practice with a partner.

1. A How much are **those / this** earrings?
   B **This / These**? They're $80.
2. A And the ring? How much is **that / those**?
   B **This / These** ring is on sale.

3 Grammar *How much . . . ?; this, these; that, those* 2.43

Extra practice p. 146

How much is it?
How much is **this** scarf?
How much is **this**?
It's $49.99.

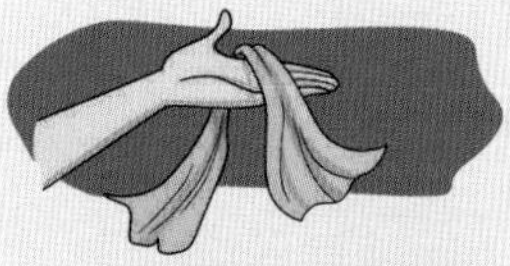

How much are they?
How much are **these** gloves?
How much are **these**?
They're $125.

How much is **that** watch?
How much is **that**?
It's $475.

How much are **those** sunglasses?
How much are **those**?
They're $50.

Saying prices

$125 = A hundred and twenty-five (dollars)

$49.99 = Forty-nine dollars and ninety-nine cents OR Forty-nine ninety-nine

In conversation

People also say *How much does it cost?* and *How much do they cost?* to talk about prices in general.

A Write questions with *How much . . . ?* and *this, that, these,* and *those*. Then practice with a partner.

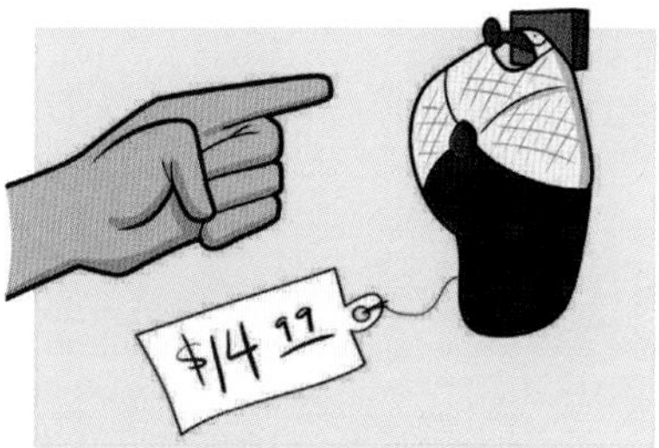

1 *How much are these green scarves?*

2 ______________________

3 ______________________

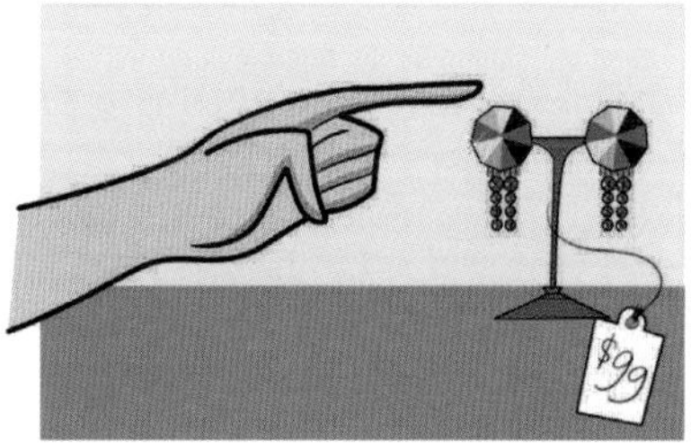

4 ______________________

5 ______________________

6 ______________________

B **Pair work** Take turns asking the questions above again. This time give your own prices.

About you **C** **Pair work** How much do you usually have to pay for the items above? Agree on an average price.

A *How much do nice scarves cost? About fifty dollars?*

B *Maybe between fifty and seventy-five dollars.*

Can I help you?

1 Conversation strategy Taking time to think

A Look at the photo. What do you think Sarah wants to buy?

B 2.44 Listen. What does Sarah buy? Who is it for?

Clerk	Can I help you?
Sarah	Uh, yes. I'm looking for a bracelet.
Clerk	All right. Is it a gift?
Sarah	Uh-huh, it's a birthday present for my sister.
Clerk	OK. And um, how much do you want to spend?
Sarah	Well, let's see . . . about $30.
Clerk	Uh-huh. Well, we have these silver bracelets here.
Sarah	Oh, they're beautiful. Um, how much is this?
Clerk	Um, it's . . . let's see . . . it's $55.95.
Sarah	Oh. That's a lot. Let me think. . . . Well, it's perfect for me. OK. I'll take it. Now, I need something for my sister!

C Notice how Sarah and the clerk say *Uh, Um, Well, Let's see,* and *Let me think* when they need time to think. Find examples in the conversation.

"Um, how much do you want to spend?"
"Well, let's see . . ."

D 2.45 Listen. Complete the conversations with the expressions in the box. There is one extra. Then practice with a partner.

Well, um	Let's see	Let me think	Uh	Um

1. A Do you like to wear jewelry?
   B ________________, I like to wear these rings and my watch. But that's it.
2. A What's your favorite store?
   B ________________, I like to shop at the mall. There are a lot of good stores there.
3. A How much do you like to spend on birthday presents?
   B ________________, I guess I spend about $15 or $20 on my friends.
4. A Where's a good place for electronics?
   B ________________. . . . Well, I like to shop online. So I'm not really sure.

About you **E** **Pair work** Ask and answer the questions above. Give your own answers. Use the expressions in the box if you need time to think.

2 Strategy plus "Conversation sounds"

Uh-huh **means *"Yes," "That's right,"* or *"I'm listening."***

Oh **shows you're surprised, happy, upset, or angry.**

In conversation

Uh-huh and ***Oh*** are in the top 50 words.

2.46 Complete the conversations using conversation sounds with the meanings given. Then listen and check. Practice with a partner.

1. A You have some money with you, right?
   B *Uh-huh* (*yes*). I have about $30.
   A ________ (*happy*) good. Can I borrow $10?
   B ________ (*upset*), not again!

2. A I have about nine or ten credit cards.
   B ________ (*surprised*), that's a lot!
   A ________ (*yes*). But I never carry cash.

3. A I have to go shopping this weekend.
   B ________ (*I'm listening*).
   A Yeah. I want to buy a tablet.
   B ________ (*surprised*), cool!

3 Listening and strategies *I'll take it.*

A 2.47 Listen to three conversations in a store. Write the price of each item.

1

2
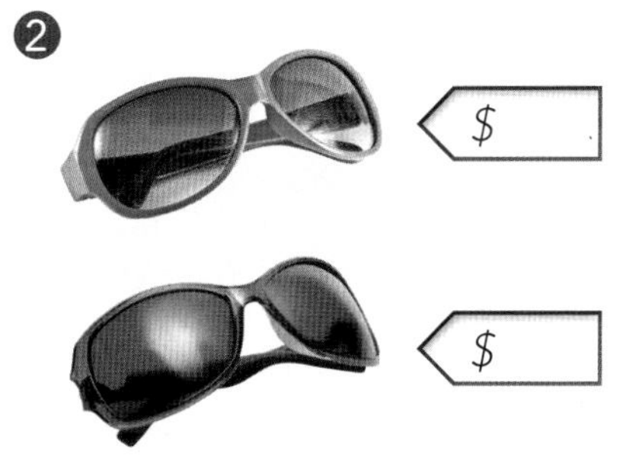

3
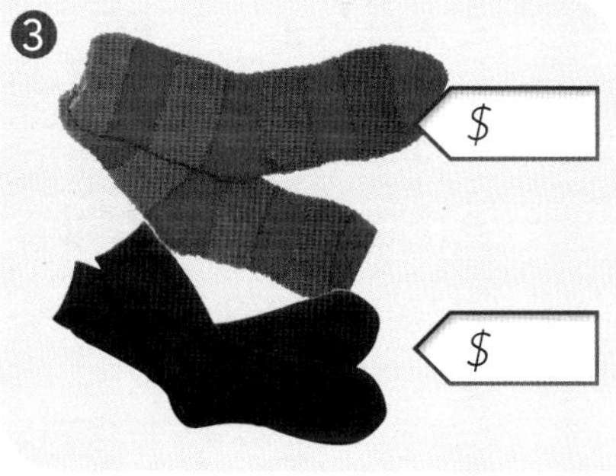

B 2.47 Listen again. Circle the items the shoppers buy. Why do they choose these items? Write a reason for each item.

About you **C Pair work Role-play the situation below. Then change roles.**

Student A: You need to buy a gift for someone very special – your wife or husband, or a girlfriend or boyfriend. You don't have a lot of money to spend.	**Student B:** You're a clerk in a store. You need to sell something. Try to sell your customer something expensive!

A Can I help you?
B Yes. I'm looking for a gift for my girlfriend.

1 Reading

A What kinds of things do people do at a mall? Make a list.

B Read the article. How many of the activities on your list are mentioned? What other things do people do at the Dubai Mall?

Reading tip

Read the title and predict six words in the article. Then scan the article to see if your words are in it.

The Dubai Mall

SHOPPING, ENTERTAINMENT, LIFESTYLE

If you want to buy a new outfit, you go to a mall. If you want to see sharks in an aquarium or listen to a world-class concert, where do you go? A mall? Well, yes. These days, malls are not just for shopping. They're an important part of our lifestyle.

SHOPPING The Dubai Mall has over a thousand stores, with everything from designer clothes to electronics. Every week, over 750,000 people – including top celebrities – shop there. There's also a *souk* – a traditional market with souvenirs, jewelry, and local craft stalls. You need to spend several days there if you want to visit every store. But that's fine because there's a 250-room luxury hotel in the mall, too.

ENTERTAINMENT There's an indoor entertainment park full of virtual reality experiences: safari rides, a snowboard jump, and other exciting games. There's an aquarium with sharks, and don't miss the amazing fountains outside – they're the height of a five-story building.

HAVE A GREAT TIME There are lots of other things to enjoy, too. Eat at one of the 160 restaurants, go and see a movie, a famous band, or piano concert, take a diving course, or just relax.

C Look at the article again. Can you find a word or an expression with these meanings?

1. one of the best in the world *world-class*
2. how you live your life ____________
3. 1,000 ____________
4. together with ____________
5. people sell things here ____________
6. some ____________
7. an expensive place to stay ____________
8. concerts, movies, games, etc. ____________
9. be sure to see ____________
10. like to do ____________

About you **D** **Pair work** Discuss the questions. Give reasons for your answers.

- Do you like to shop in large malls?
- Do you ever shop in small stores or markets?
- What kinds of stores do you like to go to?
- Is there a mall like this in your city?

2 Listening and writing Favorite places to shop

A **What's your favorite store? Why do you shop there? Tell the class.**

B 2.48 **Listen to Young-hi talk about her favorite store. Circle the correct information.**

1. There are a lot of **cool** / **expensive** stores near Young-hi's apartment.
2. Her favorite store is **a shoe store** / **a clothing store.**
3. She likes the store because they have **cheap things** / **the latest fashions.**
4. She often goes into the store **before class** / **after work.**
5. The store is open until **7:00** / **9:00.**

C **Think about your favorite store. Complete the chart.**

What's its name?	How often do you go?	What do they sell?	Why do you like it?

D **Read the Help note and the review of a store. Underline the reasons the reviewer likes the store.**

My favorite store is Bargain Basement. It's a great store because it sells designer clothes at very low prices. I usually go shopping there once a month. They sell suits, jackets, pants, sweaters, scarves, and a lot more. I like to shop there because I want to wear the latest fashions, but I don't have a lot of money.

Help note

Linking ideas with *because* to give reasons

*It's a great store **because** it sells designer clothes at very low prices.*

*I like to shop there **because** I want to wear the latest fashions.*

E **Use your notes above to write a review of your favorite store. Use *because* to give reasons. Then read your classmates' reviews. How many different stores do you learn about?**

3 Talk about it What kind of shopper are you?

Group work Discuss the questions. How are your shopping habits the same? How are they different? Tell the class.

- Do you like to go shopping? How often do you go?
- What else do you do on your shopping trips? Do you go to a café or see a movie?
- Do you enjoy window-shopping? Where do you like to go?
- Which stores have the best bargains?
- Do you buy things online? Which sites do you use?
- Do you ever buy things you don't need?
- Do you ever spend too much money?

"José and I both like to go shopping. We go shopping every weekend."

Sounds right p. 138   Free talk p. 133

Learning tip *Labeling pictures*

To learn new vocabulary, you can label pictures in books, magazines, or catalogs.

In conversation

It's black and white!

Here are the top ten colors people talk about.

1. white	6. green
2. black	7. yellow
3. red	8. gray
4. blue	9. pink
5. brown	10. orange

1 **Label the clothing and accessories in this picture.**

2 **Find and label at least three pictures you like from a magazine or catalog.**

On your own

Go into a big clothing store. How many things can you name in English?

Can Do! Now I can . . .

✓ I can . . .   ? I need to review how to . . .

- ☐ talk about clothes and accessories.
- ☐ say what I like, want, need, and have to do.
- ☐ ask for prices of things in stores.
- ☐ discuss my shopping habits.
- ☐ take time to think.
- ☐ show that I'm listening and show my feelings.
- ☐ understand conversations about prices.
- ☐ understand a conversation about shopping habits.
- ☐ read a review of a mall.
- ☐ write a review of a store.

UNIT 9

A wide world

Can Do! In this unit, you learn how to . . .

Lesson A
- Give sightseeing information with *can* and *can't*

Lesson B
- Talk about international foods, places, and people
- Say what languages you can speak

Lesson C
- Explain words using *kind of* and *kind of like*
- Use *like* to give examples

Lesson D
- Read a travel website
- Write a paragraph for a travel website

☐ 1. take tours of castles

☐ 2. see pyramids

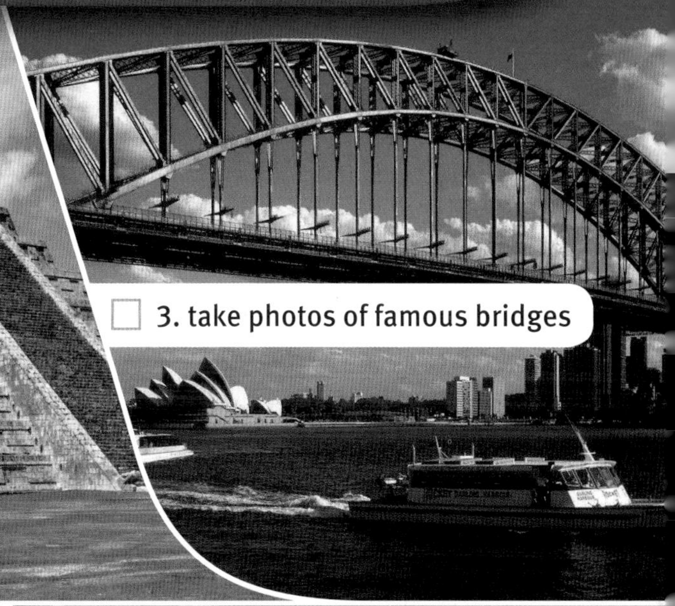

☐ 3. take photos of famous bridges

☐ 4. walk around historic districts and look at statues

☐ 5. go to the tops of towers

☐ 6. visit palaces

Before you begin . . .

Do you like to go sightseeing? Check (✓) the activities above you like to do. What other things do you like to do when you visit other places?

Lesson A Sightseeing

Emma Oh, no. It's raining! What can you do in New York on a day like this?

Ethan Oh, come on. You can do a million things. We can take a ferry to the Statue of Liberty.

Emma A ferry – in this weather?

Ethan Well, . . . we can go to the top of the Empire State Building.

Emma But you can't see anything in the rain.

Ethan Yeah, you're right. I know – let's go to a Broadway show. There are shows on Wednesday afternoons.

Emma OK. It's a deal. But first can we buy an umbrella?

Ethan Sure we can. Look, there's a store over there.

1 Getting started

A Look at the page from a guidebook. Which activities are good when it's sunny? Which are good when it's raining?

B 2.49 Listen. What do Emma and Ethan decide to do? Practice the conversation.

Figure it out **C** Circle the correct words. Use the conversation above to help you.

1. We can **to go / go to** the Statue of Liberty.
2. You can't **see / seeing** the views because it's raining.
3. What **we can / can we** do in New York on a rainy day?
4. **Do we / Can we** buy an umbrella?

About you **D** **Pair work** What are some things you can do in New York City? Take turns giving ideas.

"You can take a walk through Central Park."

2 Grammar *Can* and *can't* for possibility 2.50

Extra practice p. 147

Use *can* to talk about things that are possible. Use *can't* for things that are not possible.

I / You / He / She / We / They	**can** / **can't**	take a ferry. / see a show. / go to a museum.

What **can** you do in New York?
You **can** do a million things.

Can we buy an umbrella?
Yes, we **can.**
No, we **can't.**

In conversation

You is the most common word before *can*. *You* often means "people in general."

You can't take pictures. = *It's not possible to take pictures.*

A Match the questions and answers about New York City. Then practice with a partner.

1. Can you visit a historic neighborhood? _____
2. What kinds of museums can you go to? _____
3. Can you take a bus tour? _____
4. What can tourists do on a rainy day? _____
5. Can you visit a castle? _____
6. Where can you get a good view of the city? _____

a. You can go to the top of the Empire State Building.
b. They can go shopping or go to a Broadway show.
c. No, you can't. There are no real castles in New York.
d. Yes, you can. You can walk around Greenwich Village.
e. Well, you can go to an art museum or a history museum.
f. Yes, you can. You can take a walking tour, too.

About you **B** **Pair work** Ask the questions again, and give answers about your city.

A *Can you visit a historic neighborhood in Tokyo?*
B *Let me think. . . . Well, you can visit the Yanaka neighborhood.*

Common errors

Don't use *to* after *can*.

You ***can go*** *shopping.*
(NOT ~~*You can to go shopping.*~~)

3 Speaking naturally *Can* and *can't*

/kən/	/kən/	/kæn(t)/
What ***can*** *you do here?*	*You* ***can*** *go to the zoo.*	*You* ***can't*** *go on Mondays.*

A 2.51 Listen and repeat the sentences above. Notice the pronunciation of *can* and *can't.*

B 2.52 Listen and complete the sentences below with *can* or *can't.*

1. What fun things _________ you do in your city?
2. What _________ you do?
3. You _________ sit at outdoor cafés at night.
4. You _________ go to a show every night.
5. You _________ spend a day at the beach.
6. You _________ see live music at a club.
7. You _________ take a ferry to an island.
8. You _________ go up a tower.

About you **C** **Pair work** Are the sentences above true about your town or city? What else can and can't you do?

1 Building vocabulary and grammar

A 2.53 Listen and repeat. Check (✓) the countries you know in English. Add more.

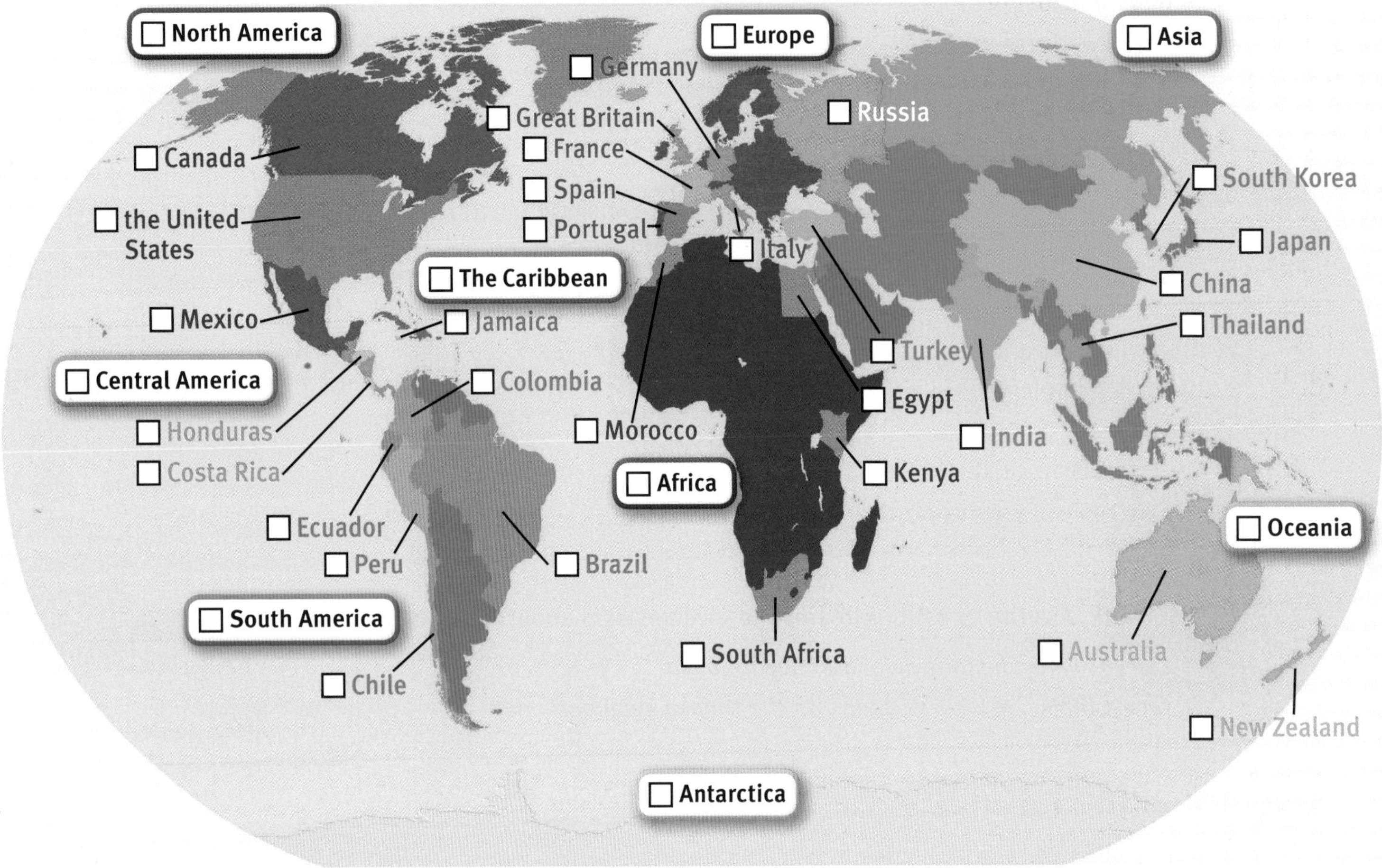

Word sort **B** Where do people speak these languages? Complete the chart. Then compare with a partner.

Arabic	Chinese	English	French	German	Hindi	Italian
Egypt						
Japanese	**Korean**	**Portuguese**	**Russian**	**Spanish**	**Turkish**	**Thai**

Vocabulary notebook p. 94

Figure it out **C** Read what Claudia says about languages. Then complete the sentences.

1. Claudia ________ speak Portuguese and English.
2. She ________ understand Spanish, but she ________ speak it.

2 Grammar *Can* and *can't* for ability 3.01

Extra practice p. 147

Use *can* to talk about things you do well. Use *can't* for things you don't do well, or don't do.

I **can** speak Chinese.	What languages **can** you speak?	**Can** you speak Spanish?
I **can't** speak Spanish.	I **can** speak English and Chinese.	Yes, I **can.** / No, I **can't.**

About you **Write questions using *can*. Then ask and answer the questions with a partner.**

1. How many / languages / you / speak? ______________________
2. you / read / the news / in English? ______________________
3. What languages / you / understand / but not speak? ______________________
4. you / understand / movies / in English? ______________________
5. you / sing / a song / in English? ______________________
6. Who / speak / English / in your family? ______________________
7. you / speak / any / other / languages? ______________________

3 Listening and speaking International dishes

A **Look at the foods below. Do you ever eat these types of food? Tell the class.**

B 3.02 **Listen to Richard make restaurant plans with a friend. Check (✓) the types of food he likes.**

☐ Brazilian

☐ Chinese

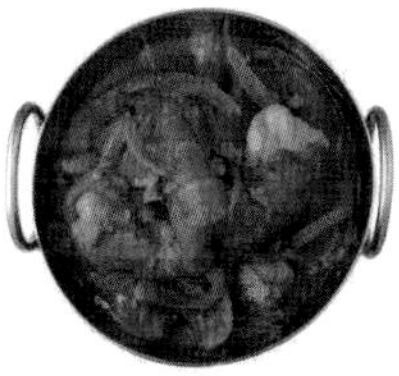

☐ Indian

☐ Italian

☐ Japanese

☐ Mexican

☐ Thai

☐ Turkish

C 3.02 **Listen again. Which restaurant do Richard and his friend choose? Why?**

About you **D** **Pair work** **Ask and answer questions about international foods. Take notes on your partner's answers. Tell the class about your partner.**

- Can you cook? What international dishes can you make?
- What are your favorite international dishes?
- What types of food don't you like?
- Can you find good international restaurants in your city?

"Ravi can cook very well. He can make Italian and French dishes."

Lesson C Conversation strategies They're a kind of candy.

1 Conversation strategy Explaining words

A How often do you order these things in a café: ice cream, soda, cake?

B 3.03 Listen. What do Yuki and Stan order?

Server	Are you ready to order?
Yuki	Yes. Can I have a large diet soda?
Server	A large diet soda?
Yuki	Yes, please.
Stan	Um, can I have coffee ice cream with chocolate sprinkles?
Server	Sure. OK.
Yuki	What are sprinkles?
Stan	They're a kind of candy. You can put them on things like ice cream and cake. They're kind of like sugar.
Yuki	Oh, I know. You can get them in Japan, too.

C Notice how Stan uses *a kind of* and *kind of like.* He's explaining a new word to Yuki. Find examples in the conversation.

"What are sprinkles?"
"They're a kind of candy."

D 3.04 Look at the photos. Complete the first sentence about each item with a word from the box. There is one extra word. Then listen and write the country each item comes from.

kimbap

a crêpe

gazpacho

lassi

bread drink dessert snack soup

1. Kimbap is a kind of ________ . It's like Japanese sushi. Kimbap is from ________ .
2. A crêpe is a kind of ________ . It's kind of like a pancake. They eat crêpes in ________ .
3. Gazpacho is a kind of ________ . It's kind of like tomato juice. It's from ________ .
4. Lassi is a kind of ________ . It's kind of like a milkshake. Lassi is from ________ .

E Pair work Take turns asking a partner to explain the words above.

"What's kimbap?" *"It's a kind of . . . "*

2 Strategy plus *Like*

You can use *like* to give examples.

In conversation

Like is one of the top 15 words.
It has other meanings:
*I **like** Brazilian food.*
*What's Thai food **like**? Spicy?*
*Sprinkles are **like** sugar.*

About you **Imagine a tourist is asking these questions about your country. Complete the answers. Then practice with a partner.**

1. A What are good souvenirs to buy?
   B Let's see. You can buy things like ________ .
2. A Do you ever see people in traditional clothes? What are they like?
   B Well, sometimes people wear things like ________ .
3. A Can you buy any traditional musical instruments?
   B Yeah, you can buy things like ________ .
4. A Where are good places to visit?
   B Well, you can visit places like ________ .

3 Listening and strategies What language is it from?

A 3.05 **Listen and complete the chart. Then match the items and the photos.**

Foreign word	What is it?	What language is it from?	Where is it popular?
1. *hamburger*	It's a kind of ________ .	________	________
2. *tortilla*	It's kind of like ________ .	________	________ and ________
3. *baklava*	It's a kind of ________ .	________	________ and ________
4. *balalaika*	It's a kind of ________ .	________	________

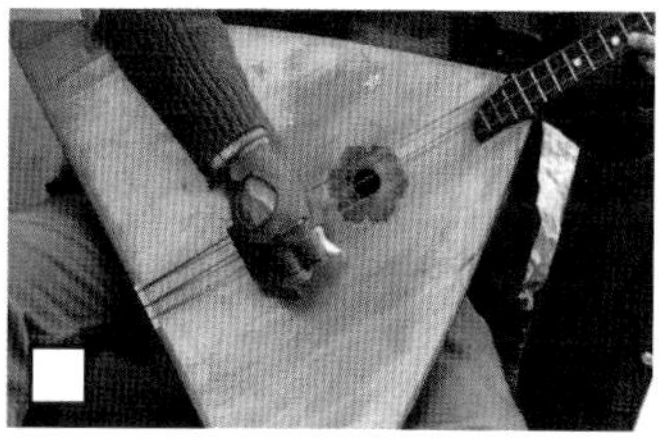
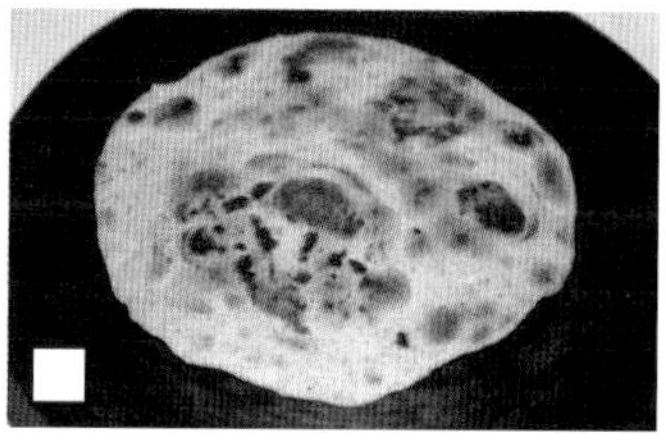

About you **B Pair work** **Imagine you are a visitor to your country. Role-play conversations. Ask your partner to explain three words (e.g., food, clothes, an instrument).**

A What's guacamole*?*
B It's a kind of snack.

Sounds right p. 138

Lesson D / Exciting destinations

1 Reading

A What do you know about these popular tourist destinations? What can you see or do there? Make a class list.

- Bogotá
- Rio de Janeiro
- Moscow
- Beijing

B Look at the website. How many of your ideas are mentioned?

Reading tip

Before you read something, think, "What do I know about this?" and "What can I learn?"

http://www.travelguide. . .

The Travel Guide

Where can you go for a great city break? Paris? London? New York? Of course! But there are many more amazing cities to see! Click More to find out about these exciting destinations.

BOGOTÁ, Colombia

Bogotá is a city of contrasts. Walk around La Candelaria, a historic neighborhood with narrow streets, old churches, and modern skyscrapers! Or go to the Chapinero neighborhood, with its beautiful park, great cafés, and shops. Don't miss the Gold Museum and its beautiful jewelry exhibits. More

MOSCOW, Russia

The Kremlin Palace and the Cathedral of Saint Basil in Red Square are just some of the historic sites you can see in Russia's capital. There are also tourist attractions *under* the city! The Moscow Metro (the subway) is full of art, statues, and crystal chandeliers. More

RIO DE JANEIRO, Brazil

Rio is famous for its beaches, mountains, and natural beauty. Walk through Tijuca National Park, or take the cable car to the top of Sugar Loaf Mountain for amazing views of the city. Or you can join the locals and head for the beach. More

BEIJING, China

In Beijing, you can experience the old and the new. Take a tour of the Forbidden City with its 600-year-old palaces. Then visit the modern Olympic "bird's nest" stadium [Beijing National Stadium]. End the day with a traditional foot massage. More

C **Look at the website again. Find these things and answer the questions. Then discuss with a partner.**

- a historic neighborhood. What are the streets like?
- two cities with palaces. Where are these palaces?
- a place to get a great view. How do you get to the top?
- a city you want to visit. What do you like about this city?

2 Talk about it Do you want to take a trip?

Group work What ideas do you and your classmates have about travel?

Can you agree on . . .

- three countries you all want to go to?
- three tourist attractions you want to see?
- three types of food you all want to try?
- two languages you need when you travel abroad?
- three really good souvenirs to buy?
- the three best places to visit in your country?

A ***Well, I want to go to Egypt.***

B ***Yeah. You can see the Pyramids.***

C ***Yes, it looks interesting, and I can speak Arabic.***

3 Writing An online travel guide

A **Read the extract below from a travel guide website. Notice how commas separate the different items in a list. Can you find similar lists on the website on page 92?**

Bangkok, Thailand is famous for its palaces, temples, and beautiful river. Visit the beautiful Grand Palace. Walk around the historic temples, the quiet gardens, and the museum. Then you can take a boat trip on the river and enjoy the sunset.

Help note

Commas in lists

*Bangkok is famous for its **palaces, temples, and beautiful river.***

B **Write about a place you know for the Travel Guide on page 92. Use the Travel Guide and the extract about Bangkok to help you.**

C **Pair work Read your classmates' paragraphs. Which ones are the most interesting?**

About you **D** **Pair work Find words in the Travel Guide with the meanings below. Then take turns using the words in sentences about your city.**

1. different things ________
2. tall buildings ________
3. the main city in a country ________
4. people who live in a place ________
5. go to ________
6. "You can't do it – it's ________."

Free talk p. 134

Vocabulary notebook

People and nations

Learning tip *Grouping vocabulary*

You can sort new vocabulary into groups. You can group nationalities by their endings and countries by their regions.

1 **Choose 15 or more nationalities you want to learn. Write them in a chart like this. Group the nationalities by their endings.**

-ese	*-ian / -an / -n*
Vietnamese	*Colombian*

-ish	Other
Spanish	*Greek*

2 **Make a chart like this for different countries.**

Africa	Asia	Europe
Morocco	*Thailand*	*France*

North America	Central America	South America

On your own

Find a world map. Label it in English. How many countries do you know?

Some countries and nationalities	
Argentina	Argentine
Brazil	Brazilian
Canada	Canadian
Chile	Chilean
China	Chinese
Colombia	Colombian
Costa Rica	Costa Rican
Ecuador	Ecuadorian
Egypt	Egyptian
France	French
Germany	German
Great Britain	British
Greece	Greek
Iraq	Iraqi
Israel	Israeli
Italy	Italian
Jamaica	Jamaican
Japan	Japanese
Mexico	Mexican
Morocco	Moroccan
Panama	Panamanian
Peru	Peruvian
Poland	Polish
Portugal	Portuguese
Russia	Russian
Saudi Arabia	Saudi
South Korea	South Korean
Spain	Spanish
Thailand	Thai
Turkey	Turkish
United Arab Emirates	Emirati
Venezuela	Venezuelan
Vietnam	Vietnamese

Can Do! Now I can . . .

✓ I can . . . ? I need to review how to . . .

- ☐ give sightseeing information.
- ☐ say what languages I can speak.
- ☐ talk about countries and nationalities.
- ☐ explain words and give examples.
- ☐ understand people making restaurant plans.
- ☐ understand explanations of foreign words.
- ☐ read a travel website.
- ☐ write a paragraph for a travel website.

1 Questions and follow-up questions!

A Complete the questions with verbs. Then match the questions and answers. Practice with a partner.

1. What _are_ you _wearing_ today? (wear) _d_
2. What colors ________ the teacher ________ today? (wear) ____
3. What ________ in your neighborhood this week? (happen) ____
4. What can you ________ in your neighborhood after midnight? (do) Can you ________ dancing? (go) ____
5. What do you want ________ tonight? (do) ____
6. What kinds of restaurants do you like ________ to? (go) ____
7. What languages can you ________? (speak) ____
8. What do you have ________ next weekend? (do) ____
9. What time do you have ________ tomorrow? (get up) ____
10. What ________ your friends ________ today? (do) ____
11. How often do you like ________ your family? (see) ____
12. What ________ you ________ about right now? (think) ____

a. There's a rock concert.
b. I want to stay home.
c. Every weekend.
d. Jeans and a T-shirt.
e. Food. I'm hungry.
f. Blue and gray.
g. English and a little Spanish.
h. They're all working.
i. I need to clean the house.
j. Well, I like Thai and Italian food.
k. No, you can't, but you can see a movie.
l. Early. I have to be at work before 8:00.

B Pair work **Choose five questions and start conversations. Ask follow-up questions. How many follow-up questions can you ask for each topic?**

A *What do you want to do tonight?*
B *I want to see a movie.*
A *Good idea! Do you know what movies are out?*
B *No, but we can look online.*

2 Play a word game.

Complete the chart. Write a word for each category beginning with each letter. You have two minutes! Then compare with a partner. Who has a word in every space?

Category	B	G	R	S	T
a sport or type of exercise	*basketball*				
a country		*Greece*			
a nationality			*Russian*		
an item of clothing or jewelry				*a suit*	
a color					*turquoise*

A *What sport begins with "B"? I have "basketball."*
B *Let's see. I have "baseball."*
A *OK, what country begins with "B"?*

3 Can you use these expressions?

Complete the conversation. Use the expressions in the box. Sometimes there's more than one correct answer. Then practice with a partner.

this	those	kind of like	Let me think	✓That's great
that	like	a kind of	Let's see	That's too bad

Samir Grant! What are you doing here?
Grant I'm working here for the summer.
Samir Wow! *That's great*. Hey, I like your uniform. I mean, ________ shirt is cool.
Grant Yeah, but I can't stand ________ hat. It's so hot.
Samir ________. Do you have to wear it?
Grant Uh-huh. So, what can I get for you?
Samir ________.... What do you have?
Grant Um . . . we have things ________ ice cream, frozen yogurt, smoothies. . . .
Samir What's a smoothie?
Grant It's ________ drink. It's ________ a milkshake.
Samir ________. Do I want frozen yogurt or a smoothie?
Grant Well, they're both good.
Samir Hey, do people really buy ________ hats?
Grant Actually, they're free with the frozen yogurt.
Samir In that case, can I have a smoothie?

4 Do you have similar interests and tastes?

A Complete the sentences in the chart with your own information.

Sports	Countries and languages
I don't like to watch ________. I want to learn (to) ________.	I want to go to ________. I want to learn ________.
Colors	**Clothes**
I like to wear ________. I can't wear ________.	I never wear ________. I wear ________ a lot.
Seasons	**Weather**
I love the ________. I don't like the ________.	I hate to go out when it ________. I love to be outside when it ________.

B Group work Compare sentences. What do you have in common?

A *I don't like to watch golf on TV.*
B *Me neither. I think it's boring.*
C *Really? I love to watch golf. But I don't like to watch baseball.*

UNIT 10

Busy lives

Can Do! In this unit, you learn how to . . .

Lesson A
- Talk about last night using simple past regular verbs

Lesson B
- Describe the past week using simple past irregular verbs
- Ask simple past *yes-no* questions

Lesson C
- Respond to news with *Good for you*, etc.
- Say *You did?* to show surprise or interest

Lesson D
- Read about a blogger's week
- Write a blog about your week, using *after, before, when,* and *then*

Before you begin . . .

What do you do during the week? Are you busy? Do you do these things? What else do you do?

- practice a musical instrument
- go grocery shopping and run errands
- work late
- cook dinner every night

WE ASKED PEOPLE . . .

What did you do last night?

1 Getting started

A What do you do on a typical weeknight at home? Tell the class.

B 3.06 Listen and read. Which of the people above had fun last night?

Figure it out **C** Find the verbs the people use to talk about last night and complete the sentences. Then circle other verbs the people use to talk about the past.

1. Peter and his wife ________ a movie. Peter ________ like it.
2. Melissa and her friends ________ dinner. She ________ want to go out.
3. Rachel ________ late. She ________ watch a movie.

2 Grammar Simple past statements – regular verbs 3.07

Extra practice p. 148

Simple past regular verbs are verb + *-ed*. The negative form is *didn't* + verb.

I	**played**	a video game.	I	**didn't play**	chess.
You	**studied**	math.	You	**didn't study**	English.
He	**watched**	a movie.	He	**didn't watch**	TV.
She	**wanted**	to stay home.	She	**didn't want**	to go out.
We	**cooked**	Italian food.	We	**didn't cook**	Chinese food.
They	**chatted**	online.	They	**didn't chat**	very long.

didn't = did not

Simple past endings

watch ▶ watch**ed**
invite ▶ invit**ed**
play ▶ play**ed**
study ▶ studi**ed**
chat ▶ chatt**ed**

In conversation

People use the simple present and simple past more often than any other verb form.

A **Complete the sentences about last night with the simple past form of the verbs.**

1. I *played* (play) a video game.
2. I ________ (not / want) to work.
3. My best friend ________ (call) me. We ________ (chat) for a while.
4. It ________ (rain), so I ________ (not / want) to go out.
5. My friend and I ________ (practice) guitar together.
6. I ________ (try) to study, but some friends ________ (call) and they ________ (invite) me to a party.
7. Some friends and I ________ (cook) dinner together.
8. I ________ (watch) a movie, but I ________ (not / like) it much.

About you **B** **Pair work** **Make the sentences above true for you.**

A ***I didn't play a video game last night. How about you?***
B ***Me neither. I watched TV.***

Common errors

Don't use a simple past form after *didn't*.

I ***didn't clean*** *the house.*
(NOT ~~*I didn't cleaned*~~ *the house.*)

3 Speaking naturally *-ed* endings

/t/ *I work**ed** on Saturday.* /d/ *We play**ed** a game.* /ɪd/ *I chatt**ed** online.*

A 3.08 **Listen and repeat the sentences above. Notice the *-ed* endings of the verbs.**

B 3.09 **Listen and repeat the verbs and sentences below. Which verbs end in /t/ or /d/? Which verbs have an extra syllable and end in /ɪd/? Check (✓) the correct column.**

		/t/ **or** /d/	/ɪd/
1. talked	I talked to some friends from college.	☑	☐
2. visited	Then I visited a classmate.	☐	☐
3. invited	She invited me over.	☐	☐
4. stayed	I stayed a couple of hours.	☐	☐
5. watched	We watched a movie together.	☐	☐
6. enjoyed	I really enjoyed my evening.	☐	☐

About you **C** **Group work** **Tell your group one thing you did each night last week. Use the verbs from the lesson. How many things do you have in common?**

"Last Sunday night I called my grandparents. How about you?"

Lesson B A busy week

1 Building vocabulary Irregular verbs

A 3.10 Listen and say the sentences. Check (✓) the things you did last week. Tell the class.

Last week . . .

1

☐ I **bought** a sweater.

2

☐ I **had** a piano lesson.

3

☐ I **made** a lot of phone calls.

4

☐ I **saw** three movies.

5

☐ I **read** a couple of books.

6

☐ I **went** to a party.

7

☐ I **took** an exam and **got** an A.

8

☐ I **met** someone interesting.

9

☐ I **did** a lot of work.
☐ I **wrote** three reports.

B Look at the verbs in bold above. Can you figure out which verbs they are? Make a list.

bought - buy

> **Note**
> Irregular simple past verbs do not end in *-ed*.
> buy ▶ bought
> *I **bought** a sweater.* (NOT ~~I buyed~~ a sweater.)

Word sort **C** Write one thing you did at each time below. Then compare with a partner.

Yesterday	Last night	Two days ago
I bought some new jeans.		
Last week	**Last month**	**Last year**

Vocabulary notebook p. 106

2 Building language

A 3.11 Listen to Mei Lei take an online survey. Check (✓) her answers.

Did you have a busy week?	Yes, I did.	No, I didn't.
1. Did you have to work late every night?	☑	☐
2. Did you write any reports?	☐	☐
3. Did you get a lot of emails?	☐	☐
4. Did you have any appointments?	☐	☐
5. Did you make a lot of phone calls?	☐	☐
6. Did you go to any meetings?	☐	☐

Figure it out **B** Complete the questions about last week. Use the survey above to help you.

1. ________ you take a class?
2. ________ you go shopping?
3. Did you ________ the laundry?
4. Did you ________ any exams?

About you **C** **Pair work** Ask and answer all the questions in Exercises 2A and 2B. How many things do you have in common?

3 Grammar Simple past *yes-no* questions 3.12

Extra practice p. 148

Did	you he / she we they	**go out** a lot last week? **play** tennis last weekend?	Yes, No,	I he / she we they	**did.** **didn't.**

About you **A** Unscramble the questions and write your own answers. Then ask and answer the questions with a partner. Remember your partner's answers.

1. you / early / go to bed / Did / last night / ?
   Did you go to bed early last night? Yes, I did. I went to bed at 9:00.
2. a lot of homework / you / Did / yesterday / do / ?
   ____
3. do any errands / you / have to / Did / last weekend / ?
   ____
4. have / Did / last month / a busy schedule / you / ?
   ____
5. last Friday / go out / Did / you and your friends / ?
   ____
6. anything interesting / your best friend / do / Did / last week / ?
   ____

About you **B** **Pair work** Find a new partner. Ask and answer questions about your first partners. How much do you remember?

A *Did Alex go to bed early last night?*
B *No, he didn't. He went to bed after midnight.*

Congratulations!

1 Conversation strategy Appropriate responses

A Match the questions and the expressions. Which expressions can you use when someone . . .

1. passed a test? __d__
2. has to take a test tomorrow? _____
3. failed a test? _____
4. got an A on a test? _____

a. I'm sorry to hear that.
b. Congratulations!
c. Good luck.
d. Good for you.

B 3.13 Listen. Which conversations are about good news? Which are about bad news?

1
Mark Thank goodness it's Friday.
Eve Yeah. I'm exhausted.
Mark Me too. I had a cold all week.
Eve You did? I'm sorry to hear that.

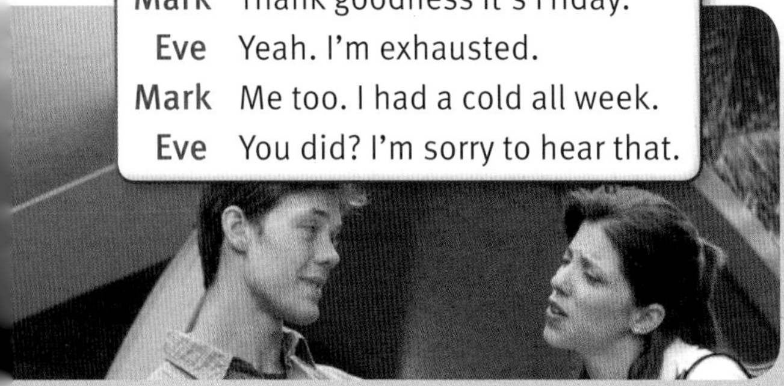

2
Selina So how did your interview at the hospital go?
Adam Great! I got the job.
Selina You did? Thank goodness! I know you really wanted it.
Adam Yeah. I start on Monday.
Selina That's great. Congratulations!

3
Celia Hey – happy birthday! Did you have a nice day?
Hugo Yeah. Thanks. I went out for lunch with some friends.
Celia You did? Nice.

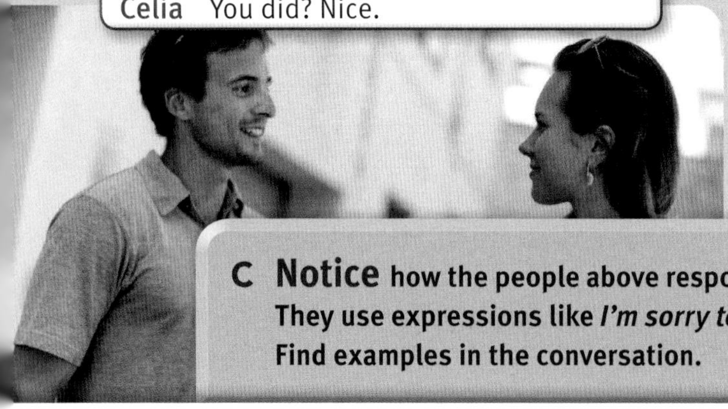

4
Olivia Did you take your driver's test yesterday?
Jake Yeah. I failed.
Olivia Oh, you did? I'm sorry to hear that.
Jake I can take it again next month, though.
Olivia Yeah? Well, good luck!

C Notice how the people above respond to news. They use expressions like *I'm sorry to hear that.* Find examples in the conversation.

"I had a cold all week."
"I'm sorry to hear that!"

D Write a response for each comment. Use the ideas in the box. Then practice with a partner.

1. I have a job interview this week. ______________________
2. I'm exhausted. I have a terrible cold. ______________________
3. I lost my job last week. ______________________
4. I'm 21 today! ______________________
5. I passed my driver's test last week. ______________________
6. My sister had to go to the hospital, but she's OK. ______________________

Good luck!
Happy birthday!
Congratulations!
I'm sorry to hear that.
Thank goodness!

"I have a job interview this week." *"That's great. Good luck!"*

2 Strategy plus *You did?*

You can say *You did?* to show that you're interested or surprised, or just that you're listening.

In conversation

You can also say ***Did you?*** to show that you're listening.

A 3.14 **Match each comment with a response. Write *a* to *e*. Then listen and check. Practice and continue the conversations with a partner.**

1. I had a nice, relaxing day at the beach last weekend. ____
2. I went to a new jazz club last Saturday. ____
3. I invited some friends over to my house last Friday night. ____
4. I stayed home on Sunday. ____
5. I took my sister to a movie for her birthday. ____

a. You did? Did you like the music?
b. Did you? Did you do chores?
c. You did? Did you go swimming?
d. Did you? Did you see anything good?
e. You did? Nice. Did you cook dinner?

About you **B Pair work** **Tell a partner three things you did last weekend. Respond with *You did?* or *Did you?* and a follow-up question.**

3 Listening and strategies Good week? Bad week?

A 3.15 **Listen to the conversations. What kind of week did the people have? Check (✓) the correct words.**

1. Laura:	☐ fun	☐ busy	☐ relaxing
2. Tyler:	☐ exhausting	☐ bad	☐ exciting
3. Louis:	☐ boring	☐ terrible	☐ interesting

B 3.15 **Listen again. Complete the sentences.**

1. Laura wrote a ____________ last week. She has to present it at a ____________ next week.
2. Tyler painted a picture of ____________ . ____________ bought it.
3. Louis's department store ____________ . Now he can't ____________ .

C 3.15 **Listen and respond. Choose the best response to give each person. There is one extra.**

1. Laura ____
2. Tyler ____
3. Louis ____

a. Oh, I'm sorry to hear that.
b. Did you? Well, happy birthday!
c. You did? Congratulations!
d. Really? Good for you. Well, good luck!

About you **D Pair work** **Did you have a good week or a bad week? Tell a partner. How long can you continue your conversation?**

A *I had a really good week. I had to write a big essay, but I finished it.*
B *You did? Good for you. Did you get an A?*

Lesson D / A blog

1 Reading

A Do you ever read blogs? Do you know people who write blogs? What topics do they write about? Tell the class.

B Read Martin's blog. What did he do last week? What problems did he have?

Reading tip

Writers don't always repeat the subject of two or more actions. *I invited her over, cooked . . . , and made . . .* (= I invited . . . , I cooked . . . , I made . . .)

http://www.martinblog. . .

M

Martin's Blog

SHE SAID YES!!!

SATURDAY, APRIL 28

What a *crazy* week! I forgot Sophie's birthday. I got a new job. Oh, and I *almost* didn't ask Sophie to marry me!

I bought a ring for Sophie on Saturday morning – I wanted to ask her to marry me that night. So I invited her over, cooked a special dinner, and made her favorite dessert. I felt nervous, but when she arrived, she said she had a cold and felt tired. *Not* the right mood for "Marry me." She went straight home after dinner. She didn't even eat my chocolate cake!

I had an important interview on Wednesday – I didn't get Sophie's cold, thank goodness – and I got the job! When I texted Sophie the good news, she texted back, "Let's have dinner on Friday to celebrate!"

Perfect, right? Wrong. We went to our favorite restaurant. Before the server showed us to our table, Sophie saw some friends, and we all ate together. I didn't want to ask her in front of all our friends.

After we left the restaurant, Sophie borrowed my jacket. (*Oh, no! The ring!*) She put her hands in the pockets and found the box!

"Oh, you remembered my birthday!" she said. (*Oh, no! Her birthday!*) Then she opened the box. Thinking fast, I dropped to one knee. "Happy birthday, Sophie! Will you marry me?"

POSTED BY MARTIN EMORY AT 11:11 AM

3 COMMENTS

April 28, 4:42 PM Bill Sanders said . . .

Nice save, Martin. Your post is hilarious! Also, congratulations! 🙂 You guys are great!

April 28, 5:21 PM Mike said . . .

Good luck to both of you! And happy birthday to Sophie! Call me sometime and let's talk.

April 28, 6:47 PM Sophie said . . .

You're so sweet, Martin. Don't worry – you don't need to buy me a birthday present. I love you.

C Read Martin's blog again. Are the statements true or false? Check (✓) *True* (T) or *False* (F). Compare with a partner.

		T	F
1.	Martin wanted to ask Sophie to marry him on Saturday.	☐	☐
2.	Sophie went home early on Saturday because she had a cold.	☐	☐
3.	Martin got Sophie's cold.	☐	☐
4.	Sophie felt happy when Martin got a new job.	☐	☐
5.	Martin planned a big dinner with Sophie's friends on Friday night.	☐	☐
6.	Martin bought Sophie a birthday present.	☐	☐

2 Listening and speaking *Guess what I did!*

A 3.16 **Listen to three voice mail messages. What are they about? Number the topics 1 to 3. There are two extra.**

getting in shape ____ work ____ a vacation ____ a new movie ____ studying ____

B 3.16 **Listen again. Circle the correct words to complete the sentences.**

1. Ethan ate a lot of **fast food** / **new dishes** on his trip.
2. He's learning **French** / **to cook**.
3. Alexis bought some new clothes for **her job** / **a show**.
4. She **likes to** / **doesn't like to** shop for clothes.
5. Sarah's friends think she **gets** / **doesn't get** a lot of exercise.
6. Sarah **watched TV** / **read a magazine** on her exercise bike.

About you **C** **Group work** **Think of something interesting you did recently. Prepare a voice mail message to tell a classmate. Take turns telling your messages.**

3 Writing A great day

A **Think of a day when you had a really interesting or fun experience. What different things did you do that day? Write a list. Then number the sentences in the order you did them.**

____

____

____

____

B **Read the blog entry below and the Help note. Underline the words in the blog that show the order of events. Then write a blog using your ideas from above. Use *before, after, when,* and *then*.**

A "Thank Goodness It's Friday" Party

Last Friday, I met a friend for coffee after work. We usually go out on Fridays, but we wanted to do something different. We felt exhausted, and we wanted to relax a little! Before we left the coffee shop, we called four friends. We invited them to my apartment for a little party. Then we stopped at a supermarket and bought some sodas and three big pizzas. When our friends arrived, we just sat and talked for hours. And we ate all three pizzas! We had a really great time!

Help note

Ordering events with *before, after, when,* and *then*

I met a friend ***after*** */* ***before*** *class.*

I called a friend ***before*** *I went out.*
Before *I went out, I called a friend.*

I went to bed ***when*** *I came home.*
When *I came home, I went to bed.*

I left work. ***Then*** *I met a friend.*

About you **C** **Pair work** **Read your partner's blog. Ask questions to find out more information.**

"So you sat and talked for hours. What did you talk about?"

Free talk p. 135

Sounds right p. 138

Learning tip *Making notes on verbs*

When you write down a new verb, make notes about it. Is it regular (*R*) or irregular (*Ir*)? How do you spell the different forms? How do you pronounce the endings?

Regular?	*he, she, it, -s*	*-ing form*	*Simple past*
watch (R)	*watches /ɪz/*	*watching*	*watched /t/*
take (Ir)	*takes /s/*	*taking*	*took*

1 **Make a chart like the one above. Complete it for these verbs: *study, chat, invite, do, buy,* and *meet*.**

2 **Here are the simple past forms of some irregular verbs you know. Complete the chart with the verb for each simple past form.**

eat	ate		felt		meant		saw		took
	bought		forgot		met		sent		went
	brought		found		paid		slept		went out
	came		gave		put		sold		woke up
	chose		got		ran		spent		won
	cost		had		read		spoke		wore
	did		knew		said		swam		wrote
	drank		left		sang		thought		
	drove		made		sat		told		

On your own

Before you go to sleep tonight, think of all the things you did today. How many things can you remember?

Can Do! Now I can . . .

✓ I can . . . ? I need to review how to . . .

- talk about the past.
- respond to news.
- show that I'm listening.
- understand people talk about their week.
- understand voice mail messages.
- read a blog.
- write a blog about my week.

UNIT 11

Looking back

Can Do! In this unit, you learn how to . . .

Lesson A
- Describe past experiences
- Ask and answer questions using the past of *be*

Lesson B
- Talk about vacations
- Talk about activities with *go* and *get* expressions

Lesson C
- Show interest by answering and then asking a similar question
- Use *Anyway* to change the topic or end a conversation

Lesson D
- Read a funny magazine story
- Write a story using punctuation for conversations

1. my first friend

2 .my first home

3. my first pet

Before you begin . . .
- What do you remember about these things?
- What other "firsts" do you remember?

My first . . .

1 Getting started

A **Circle the best words to complete the sentences. Are the sentences true for you?**

1. I'm pleased with my grades. I'm **happy / unhappy**.
2. I'm not relaxed in exams. I'm **nervous / happy**.
3. I often make mistakes in class. It's **embarrassing / fun**.
4. I don't talk a lot. I'm **loud / quiet**.
5. I'm 18. I'm **young / old**.
6. I hate homework. It's **fun / awful**.

B 3.17 **Listen. Why was Ryan scared? Why was Melissa nervous?**

http://www.collegepost...

The College Post

What do you remember?

We interviewed two students about some "firsts" in their lives.

Ryan Wong

The College Post: Do you remember your first teacher?

Ryan Wong: Kind of. I remember her name was Ms. Johnson and that we were all scared of her.

The College Post: Was she strict?

Ryan Wong: Yeah, she was very strict. It was awful! I was so unhappy that year – I was only five. The other kids weren't too happy either. We were all very quiet in her class.

Melissa King

The College Post: Do you remember your first job?

Melissa King: Yeah. I had a part-time job in a restaurant. I was a server. I was young – only 16. I remember that on my first day things were really busy, and I was very nervous. I made a lot of embarrassing mistakes, and my boss wasn't too pleased.

The College Post: What about the customers? Were they nice?

Melissa King: Yes, they were – I guess because I was new.

Figure it out **C** **Can you complete the answers to these questions about Ryan and Melissa? Then ask and answer the questions with a partner.**

1. A Was Ryan's class fun?
   B No, it wasn't. It ________ awful!
2. A ________ Ryan's teacher strict?
   B Yes, she was. She ________ *very* strict.
3. A Was Melissa's boss happy about her mistakes?
   B No, he ________ too pleased.
4. A ________ Melissa's customers nice?
   B Yes, they ________ , because Melissa ________ new.

2 Grammar Simple past of *be* 3.18

Extra practice p. 149

I	**was** only five.	I	**wasn't** very old.	**Were** you nervous? Yes, I **was.** / No, I **wasn't.**
He	**was** very young.	He	**wasn't** happy.	**Was** she strict? Yes, she **was.** / No, she **wasn't.**
She	**was** strict.	She	**wasn't** very nice.	**Was** it fun? Yes, it **was.** / No, it **wasn't.**
It	**was** awful.	It	**wasn't** fun.	**Were** they nice? Yes, they **were.** / No, they **weren't.**
You	**were** nervous.	You	**weren't** relaxed.	
We	**were** quiet.	We	**weren't** noisy.	
They	**were** scared.	They	**weren't** happy.	
	wasn't = was not		*weren't = were not*	

A Complete these conversations with *was, wasn't, were,* or *weren't.* Practice with a partner.

1. A Do you remember your first teacher?
   B Yeah. His name *was* Mr. Davis.
   A ________ he strict with you?
   B No, he ________ . He ________ always very nice.

Common errors

Don't use *was* with *you, we,* or *they.*

*They **were** expensive.*
(NOT ~~*They was expensive*~~.)

2. A ________ you shy when you ________ little?
   B Yeah, I ________ . I ________ scared to talk in class. It ________ awful.

3. A Tell me about your first best friend. ________ you classmates?
   B No, we ________ . She ________ in my class. We ________ neighbors.

4. A Did you have a favorite toy when you ________ a kid?
   B Yes. It ________ my train set. It ________ really cool.
   A ________ it a birthday present?
   B No, it ________ . I bought it with my own money.

About you **B Pair work** **Ask and answer the questions. Give your own answers.**

3 Speaking naturally Stress and intonation

*Were you **ner**vous?* *No, I **was**n't.* *I was re**lax**ed.*

A 3.19 **Listen and repeat the sentences above. Notice how the voice falls or rises on the stressed words.**

B 3.20 **Listen and repeat the questions and answers below about a first English class.**

1. A Was the class **eas**y? B No, it **was**n't. It was **hard**!
2. A Were the other students **good**? B Yes, they were all very **smart**.
3. A Were they **nice** to you? B Yes, they **were**. They were very **friend**ly.
4. A Was your teacher **strict**? B Yes, she **was**. But she was **nice**.

About you **C Class activity** **Interview three students about their first English class. Ask the questions above.**

Vacations

1 Building language

A 3.21 **Listen. What did Jason do on his vacation? Practice the conversation.**

Diana	Great picture! When did you get back?
Jason	Last night.
Diana	So how was your vacation?
Jason	Oh, it was wonderful.
Diana	Where did you go exactly?
Jason	We went to Hawaii.
Diana	Wow! What was the weather like?
Jason	It was hot, but not too hot.
Diana	Nice. So what did you do there?
Jason	We went to the beach every day, and I went parasailing. I didn't want to come home.
Diana	Well, I'm glad you did. . . . I have a ton of work for you!

Figure it out **B** **Circle the correct words. Then ask a partner the questions.**

1. A How **was / did** your last vacation?
   B It was wet. We didn't do much.
2. A Where did you **go / went**?
   B We went camping in Oregon.
3. A What **was the weather / the weather was** like?
   B It rained every day.
4. A What **did you / you did** do?
   B We played cards a lot.

2 Grammar Simple past information questions 3.22

Extra practice p. 149

How was your vacation?	It was fun.	**Where did** you **go**?	To Hawaii.
What was the weather like?	It was hot.	**Who did** you **go** with?	A couple of friends.
Where was Jason last week?	On vacation.	**What did** you **do**?	We went to the beach.
Where were you exactly?	In Hawaii.	**Who did** Jason **go** with?	His family.
How long were you there?	A week.	**When did** they **get** back?	Last night.

About you **Write questions for these answers. Then practice with a partner. Practice again, giving your own answers.**

1. *How was your last vacation*? It was great.
2. ______________________? I went to Greece.
3. ______________________? Wonderful. It was sunny every day.
4. ______________________? My brother and sister.
5. ______________________? We were there for a week.
6. ______________________? We saw the Parthenon in Athens.

"How was your last vacation?" *"It was OK. I stayed here in the city."*

Sounds right p. 138

3 Building vocabulary

A 3.23 **Listen to these memories of trips. Match the memories with the pictures.**

1 "I **went hiking** with a friend in Peru, and we **got lost**. We **got** really scared when it **got** dark."

2 "I **got** a new camera from my mom for my trip to Africa."

3 "I **got sick** on our honeymoon, right after we **got married**."

4 "I **went on a trip** across Canada with a friend. It was awful. We didn't **get along**."

5 "I **went to see** a band in Miami. I met the lead singer, and **I got his autograph**."

6 "I **went snorkeling** in Thailand. It was great, but I **got a bad sunburn**."

Word sort **B** **Make word webs for *get* and *go* with expressions from the sentences above. Add ideas.**

go hiking — go

get lost — get

About you **C** **Pair work** **Tell your partner about your best trip or vacation. What did you do?**

A *Last year I went hiking with my cousin.*

B *You did? Where did you go? Was it fun?*

Vocabulary notebook p. 116

Anyway, what did *you* do?

1 Conversation strategy Answer a question; then ask a similar one.

A What questions can you ask your friends about their weekend? Make a list.

B 3.24 Listen. How was Jessica's weekend? How was Tom's weekend?

Tom	So, how was your weekend, Jessica?
Jessica	Great! Gina and I went biking out in the country.
Tom	Oh, really?
Jessica	Yeah, it was fun, but there were lots of hills. I was exhausted by the end of the day.
Tom	Yeah, I bet.
Jessica	So . . . anyway, what did *you* do?
Tom	Oh, I had a party Saturday. It was good.
Jessica	Really? Nice.
Tom	Well, anyway, . . . I have to go. I have a meeting now. See you later.

C Notice how Jessica answers Tom's question and then asks a similar one. She shows she is interested in Tom's news, too. Find her question in the conversation.

About you **D** Answer each question. Then think of a similar question to ask. Practice your conversations with a partner.

1. A How was your weekend? Was it good?
   B *Answer:* ______________________________
   Then ask: ______________________________

2. A What did you do on Friday night?
   B *Answer:* ______________________________
   Then ask: ______________________________

3. A Did you do anything fun on Sunday?
   B *Answer:* ______________________________
   Then ask: ______________________________

2 Strategy plus *Anyway*

You can use *Anyway* to change the topic of a conversation.

You can also use *Anyway* to end a conversation.

In conversation

Anyway is one of the top 300 words.

3.25 Listen to the conversations. Why are these people saying *anyway*? Circle *a* or *b*. Then practice with a partner.

1. A What did you do on Saturday?
   B Not much. I slept late, went shopping. It was OK. But **anyway,** do you want to go out tonight?
   a. to change the topic
   b. to end the conversation
2. A Did you work last weekend?
   B Yeah. I had to study for an exam. I got so tired. But, **anyway,** I got a new phone last week.
   a. to change the topic
   b. to end the conversation
3. A Where were you on Sunday evening?
   B Oh, I was out. I went bowling. . . . Well, **anyway,** it's late. See you tomorrow.
   a. to change the topic
   b. to end the conversation

3 Listening and strategies Weekend fun

A **3.26 Listen to three conversations. Which three topics do the people talk about in each conversation? Number the topics 1, 2, or 3.**

☐ biking	☐ the movies	☐ the beach	☐ dancing	☐ a party
☐ shopping	☐ studying	☐ hiking	☐ a concert	☐ a road trip

B **3.26 Listen again. Answer the questions about each conversation.**

Conversation 1 a. What was the weather like in the mountains? ____________________
b. What did Rex do on the weekend? ____________________

Conversation 2 a. What did Laura buy? ____________________
b. What did John do? Was he home late? ____________________

Conversation 3 a. What didn't Emma do last weekend? ____________________
b. Why does Joe have to go? ____________________

C **3.26 Listen again. Check (✓) the conversations that end.**

☐ Conversation 1 ☐ Conversation 2 ☐ Conversation 3

About you **D** **Class activity** **Start a conversation about last weekend with a classmate. End your conversation, and then talk with another classmate. Talk to at least three people.**

1 Reading

A **Do you ever read the letters people send in to magazines? What topics do people write about? Add ideas.**

problems, funny stories . . .

Reading tip

As you read a story, stop at the end of each paragraph. Can you guess what happens next?

B **Read the story from a magazine. What kind of story is it? What happened to Sarah?**

Our community:

This week – funny stories from our readers

How embarrassing!

By Sarah Morgan

A funny thing happened to me yesterday after work. I was really hungry and I didn't feel like making dinner, so I went to a fast-food place near my office building. I got a cheeseburger, some fries, and a soda. The restaurant was really crowded, so I had to share a table. I sat down with my tray across from a young guy. I said, "Hi. Is this seat free?" He nodded and smiled, but he didn't say anything. He seemed pretty nice.

Anyway, I got out a magazine and started eating my burger. It was a really interesting article and I couldn't stop reading. But then I saw the guy take one of my fries! I couldn't believe it, but I was too embarrassed to say anything. Then he took another one, and I still didn't say anything!

Then I thought, "Those are my fries." So I took a handful and ate them. The guy looked at me in a funny way, but he didn't say anything. Then he did it again and ate another one of my fries! It was really strange.

Finally, a few minutes later, he got up, took his tray, and left. That's when I realized the fries were on his tray! And my fries? They were under my magazine. How embarrassing! I ran out into the street. There was the guy.

Continued on next page . . .

C **Read Sarah's story again. Then match the two parts of each sentence.**

1. Sarah had dinner at a fast-food place because _h_
2. The restaurant was crowded, so ____
3. Before Sarah sat down at the young guy's table, ____
4. Sarah was surprised when the guy ate some fries because ____
5. Sarah didn't say anything about the fries because ____
6. The guy gave Sarah a funny look when ____
7. When the guy left the table with the fries on his tray, ____
8. When Sarah looked under her magazine, ____

a. she realized they were *his* fries.
b. she was very embarrassed.
c. she found her own fries.
d. she had to sit with someone.
e. she said, "Hi. Is this seat free?"
f. she thought they were *her* fries.
g. she started eating some fries.
h. she didn't want to cook.

2 Writing He said, she said

A Read the Help note and Sarah's story again. Notice the punctuation. Then add punctuation to the rest of her story below.

Continued from previous page . . .

"Hi. We
I said, "~~hi. we~~ met a few minutes ago."
He said yeah, we did.
I said I think I ate your fries.
He laughed and said yes, you did.
I apologized and said I thought they were my fries.
He said that's OK. No problem.
I said can I buy some more fries for you.
He laughed and said thank you I'm still a little hungry.

Help note

Punctuation with speech

- Use quotation marks (" ") around the things people say.
- Use a comma (,) after ***said.***
- Use a capital letter to start a quotation.

*I said, **"I**s this seat free?"*
*He said, **"S**ure."*

B What did they say next? Write six sentences to finish the story. Be sure to use the correct punctuation for things people say. Read your ending to the class.

3 Listening and speaking Funny stories

A 3.27 Listen to Miranda and John tell part of a story. Circle the correct information.

I did something really embarrassing about a month ago. . . .

I said something once to a dinner guest. . . .

1. Miranda was **at work** / **in a store.**
2. Her friend **loves** / **hates** shopping.
3. They looked at a **dress** / **sweater.**
4. Miranda **liked** / **didn't like** the colors.
5. John was **10** / **20** years old.
6. His father's **boss** / **friend** came for dinner.
7. John and the man talked about **school** / **work.**
8. John **liked** / **didn't like** his new teacher.

B 3.28 Choose the best ending for each story. Circle *a* or *b*. Then listen and check your guesses.

1. Miranda's story
   a. Then my friend said, "Actually, I bought one last week."
   b. The clerk said, "Do you like this season's colors?"
2. John's story
   a. My teacher said, "You look tired. Were you up late last night?"
   b. My teacher said, "I hear you met my father last night."

About you **C Pair work** **Retell one of the stories above to a partner, or tell a funny story of your own.**

Free talk p. 135

Learning tip *Time charts*

You can use a time chart to log new vocabulary. Look at the example below.

1 Complete the sentences on the time chart with the correct verbs from the box. You can use a verb more than once.

bought	had	took	didn't have	went
got	✓lived	was	didn't get along	

Time in the past	Event or experience
15 years ago	My family *lived* in Hawaii.
10 years ago	I ________ in high school.
5 years ago	I ________ my driver's license and ________ my first car.
2–4 years ago	I ________ my first trip abroad.
last year	I ________ sick and ________ in the hospital for two weeks.
last month	My brother ________ married and ________ to Fiji on his honeymoon.
last week	My friend Jo ________ a party. It ________ boring. I ________ a good time.
last weekend	I ________ hiking with a friend. It was awful – we ________ .

2 Make a time chart like the one above. Write about your past experiences.

On your own

Make a time chart, and put it on your wall. Look at it every day.

Can Do! Now I can . . .

✓ I can . . . ? I need to review how to . . .

- ☐ describe past school, work, and travel experiences.
- ☐ talk about activities with *go* and *get* expressions.
- ☐ show interest by answering then asking a question.
- ☐ change the topic or end a conversation.
- ☐ understand conversations about weekends.
- ☐ understand people telling funny stories.
- ☐ read a funny magazine story.
- ☐ write a story that includes conversations.

UNIT 12

Fabulous food

Can Do! In this unit, you learn how to . . .

Lesson A
- Talk about eating habits using countable and uncountable nouns, *How much,* and *How many*

Lesson B
- Talk about food
- Make offers using *Would you like . . .* and *some* or *any*

Lesson C
- Use *or something* and *or anything* in lists
- End *yes-no* questions with *or . . . ?* to be less direct

Lesson D
- Read a restaurant guide
- Write a restaurant review

Before you begin . . .

Match the pictures with the food categories. Which foods did you eat yesterday?

- ☐ **grains:** bread, rice, and pasta
- 1 **dairy:** milk and cheese
- ☐ **seafood:** fish and shellfish
- ☐ **meat:** beef and chicken
- ☐ **vegetables:** broccoli and carrots
- ☐ **fruit:** bananas and a papaya

1 Getting started

A What are some foods that the people below don't eat? Make a list.

- a vegetarian
- a "picky" eater
- a person on a diet
- a person with food allergies

B 3.29 Listen. Ellen is leaving a message for her parents. What is her problem? Which plate of food does Ellen think is right for Amy? for Juan? for David?

Figure it out **C** Find the food words in Ellen's message. Are they singular or plural? Write them in the chart. Then circle *a lot of*, *much*, and *many*. Do singular or plural nouns follow the words?

Singular			Plural		
meat			*eggs*		

About you **D** **Pair work** Which of the foods above do you like? Which don't you like? Tell a partner.

A *I love meat. How about you?*

B *Um, I don't eat meat, but I like fish and vegetables.*

2 Grammar Countable / uncountable nouns 3.30

Extra practice p. 150

Countable nouns	Uncountable nouns
Examples: an apple, six potatoes	Examples: cheese, meat, fish
Use *a* / *an* or plural *-s*:	**Don't use *a* / *an* or plural *-s*:**
I have **an egg** for breakfast every day.	I drink **milk** every morning.
I don't eat **bananas.**	I don't eat **seafood.**
Use *how many, a lot of,* and *many*:	**Use *how much, a lot of,* and *much*:**
How many eggs do you eat a week?	**How much milk** do you drink a day?
I eat **a lot of eggs.**	I drink **a lot of milk.**
I don't eat **a lot of eggs.**	I don't drink **a lot of milk.**
I don't eat **many** (**eggs**).	I don't drink **much** (**milk**).

A Circle the correct words in these conversations. Then practice with a partner.

1. A How **much / many** fruit do you eat a day?
   B Well, I have **banana / a banana** every day for breakfast, and I eat **much / a lot of** fruit after dinner for dessert.
2. A How **much / many** times a week do you eat **potato / potatoes**?
   B About once a week. But I eat **rice / the rice** every day.
3. A Do you eat **many / a lot of** red meat? Or do you prefer **chicken / the chicken**?
   B Actually, I'm a vegetarian, so I never eat **meat / meats**.
4. A How often do you eat **seafood / the seafood**?
   B Well, I eat **much / a lot of** fish, but I'm allergic to **shellfish / a shellfish**.
5. A How **much / many** eggs do you eat a week?
   B I don't eat **much / many.** I don't really like **egg / eggs**.
6. A How often do you eat **vegetable / vegetables**?
   B I usually eat **much / a lot of** French fries. Is that a vegetable?

Common errors

Don't use *the* before nouns to talk about food in general.

I don't like meat, but I eat eggs. (NOT ~~*I don't like the meat, but I eat the eggs*~~.)

About you **B** **Pair work** Ask and answer the questions. Give your own answers.

3 Talk about it What's your diet?

Group work Discuss the questions. Do you have similar habits? Then tell the class one interesting thing about a person in your group.

- Are you a picky eater? What foods do you hate?
- Are you allergic to any kinds of food? What are you allergic to?
- Are you on a special diet? What can't you eat?
- How many times a day do you eat?
- Do you ever skip meals?
- In your opinion, what foods are good for you? What foods aren't?
- Do you have any bad eating habits? What are they?

1 Building vocabulary

A 3.31 **Listen and say the words. Which foods do you like? Which don't you like? Tell the class.**

Word sort **B** **Complete the chart with the foods above. Add ideas. Then tell a partner about your diet.**

meat	seafood	vegetables	fruit	dairy	grains	drinks	snacks	other
lamb	*clams*							

"I eat a lot of lamb." *"I don't eat many clams."* *"I don't eat much ice cream."*

Vocabulary notebook p. 126

2 Building language

A 3.32 **Listen. What do Ted and Phil have to do before dinner? Practice the conversation.**

Ted I guess it's my turn to cook dinner. So what would you like?

Phil Um, I'd like some chicken. Do we have any?

Ted Um, no, we need to get some. We don't have any vegetables, either. Would you like to go out for pizza?

Phil Again? No, I think I'd like to stay home tonight.

Ted OK. Then we have to go to the grocery store.

Phil Well, I went grocery shopping last week. I think it's your turn.

Figure it out **B** **Circle the correct words. Then practice with a partner.**

1. A What would you **like / like to** eat?
   B I'd **like / like to** some chicken.
2. A I'd like **some / any** fish.
   B We don't have **some / any.** Let's go buy **some / any.**

3 Grammar *Would like; some* and *any* 3.33

Extra practice p. 150

Use *would like* + *to* + verb or *would like* + noun.

Would you **like to** go out?
No, I'**d like to** stay home.

What **would** you **like** for dinner?
I'**d like** some chicken.

Would you **like** some tea?
Yes, please. / No, thanks.

I'd = I would

Use *some* in affirmative statements and *any* in questions and negative statements.

Do we have **any** vegetables?
Yes, we have **some** (vegetables).
No, we don't have **any** (vegetables).

Do we have **any** chicken?
Yes, we have **some** (chicken).
No, we don't have **any** (chicken).

In conversation

Any is common in questions:
*Do you have **any** cookies?*
Some is common in questions that are offers or requests:
*Would you like **some** chicken?*
*Can I have **some** chocolate?*

A Complete the conversations. Use *some, any, would . . . like*, or *'d like*. Sometimes there are two correct answers.

1. A I'm sleepy. I'd like to go for a walk. ___Would___ you ___like___ to come?
   B Sure. Let's go out for ________ coffee. I ________ to get ________ cake, too.
2. A I'm really thirsty. Do you have ________ water with you?
   B Well, I have ________ soda. Would you like ________ ?
3. A ________ you ________ a snack? I have ________ cookies and peanuts. Oh wait, I don't have ________ peanuts.
   B Um, I ________ some fruit. Do you have ________ ?
4. A What ________ you ________ to do after class? Do you have ________ plans?
   B Well, I need to go shopping and get ________ food.
   A Oh, I can come with you. I need to get ________ milk, too. I don't have ________ .

About you **B Pair work** **Ask and answer the questions. Give your own answers.**

*A **I'm sleepy. I'd like to go for a walk. Would you like to come?***
*B **Sure. Let's get some soda, too.***

Common errors

Always add *to* when *I'd like* is followed by a verb.

***I'd like to go** for a walk.*
(NOT ~~*I'd like go for a walk*~~.)

4 Speaking naturally *Would you . . . ?*

*What **would you** like?* *Would you like a snack?* ***Would you** like to have dinner?*

A 3.34 **Listen and repeat the questions above. Notice the pronunciation of *Would you . . . ?***

B 3.35 **Listen and complete the questions. Then listen again and practice.**

1. What would you like to ____________ ?
2. Would you like to ____________ ?
3. Would you like to ____________ ?
4. Where would you like to ____________ ?
5. What would you like to ____________ ?

About you **C Pair work** **Make dinner plans with a partner. Use the questions above.**

I just want a sandwich or something.

1 Conversation strategy *or something* and *or anything*

A What kinds of food are popular for lunch? Make a list.

B 3.36 Listen. What do Carrie and Henry decide to do for lunch?

Carrie	Let's take a break for lunch.
Henry	Sure. Would you like to go out or . . . ?
Carrie	Well, I just want a sandwich or something.
Henry	OK. I don't want a big meal or anything, either. But I'd like something hot.
Carrie	Well, there's a new Spanish place near here, and they have good soup.
Henry	That sounds good.
Carrie	OK. And I can have a sandwich or a salad or something like that.
Henry	Great. So let's go there.

C Notice how Carrie and Henry use *or something (like that)* and *or anything*. They don't need to give a long list of things. Find examples in the conversation.

"I just want a sandwich or something."

D Complete the conversations with *or something* and *or anything*. Then practice with a partner.

1. A Do you eat a big lunch?
   B No, I usually just have a salad ____________ .
2. A What do you usually have for breakfast?
   B Oh, I just have some coffee and a muffin ____________ .
   A You don't have eggs ____________ ?
3. A Would you like to go out for dinner ____________ ?
   B Sure. But I don't want a big meal ____________ . Something light maybe.
   A OK. Well, let's go somewhere with a salad bar ____________ .

Note

Use ***or something*** in affirmative statements and in questions that are offers and requests.

Use ***or anything*** in negative statements and most questions.

About you **E Pair work** Ask and answer the questions. Give your own answers.

2 Strategy plus *or . . . ?*

You can use *or . . . ?* at the end of *yes-no* questions to make them less direct.

In conversation

Or is one of the top 50 words.

About you **Pair work** Check (✓) the questions you can end with *or . . . ?* and write it in the blank. Then ask and answer all of the questions.

- [x] 1. Do you eat lunch every day *or . . .* ?
- [ ] 2. Do you make your own lunch ________ ?
- [ ] 3. Where do you usually eat ________ ?
- [ ] 4. Do you just have something light ________ ?
- [ ] 5. Would you like to have lunch sometime ________ ?
- [ ] 6. Where would you like to go ________ ?

A *Do you eat lunch every day or . . . ?*

B *Well, I never skip lunch. I usually go out and buy a sandwich or something.*

Sounds right p. 138

3 Listening and strategies *If you want my advice . . .*

A 3.37 Listen to the conversations. Complete the sentence about each person. Write *a* to *e*. There is one extra phrase.

1. Jack ____
2. Rachel ____
3. Peter ____
4. Abby ____

a. wants to buy a sandwich at a food stand.
b. doesn't usually eat anything for lunch.
c. would like a nice big omelette.
d. would like to have a big meal.
e. doesn't want pizza or anything.

B 3.37 Listen again. Do you agree with the advice that is given to the people above? Circle *I agree* or *I don't really agree*, and complete each sentence with your own view.

1. **I agree / I don't really agree.** I think that ________________________________ .
2. **I agree / I don't really agree.** I feel that ________________________________ .
3. **I agree / I don't really agree.** I think that ________________________________ .
4. **I agree / I don't really agree.** I believe that ________________________________ .

C **Pair work** Make plans to go out after class today. Discuss what kind of food you'd like. Agree on a place to go.

Free talk p. 136

A *So, would you like to go out for lunch after class, or . . . ?*

B *Sure. I don't really want a big meal or anything. So maybe a sandwich or something.*

1 Reading

A Do you know an interesting restaurant? What's special about it? Check (✓) the boxes. Then tell the class.

- ☐ It has a nice atmosphere.
- ☐ It has live music.
- ☐ It serves unusual food.
- ☐ It has a beautiful view.
- ☐ It has good service.
- ☐ other ______________

B Read the restaurant guide. Which restaurant would you like to try? Tell a partner why you'd like to go there.

Reading tip

As you read, imagine each place. Ask yourself, "Would I like to eat there?"

Restaurant Guide: Try something different!

We searched the world and found these unusual places to eat.

Chillout ice restaurant, Dubai

Would you like to visit a *really* cool restaurant? Then try this place. Everything is made of ice, from the tables and chairs to the pictures on the walls. When you order a soda, it comes in an ice glass, and your meal is served on an ice plate. Luckily, if you get too cold, you can ask for a warm blanket and some hot chocolate. Be sure to try some ice cream, too. It never melts!

Dinner in the Sky, in over 35 countries

How would you like to dine 50 meters (164 feet) above your favorite view? Then hire Dinner in the Sky for a special event. You and 21 guests can enjoy dinner at a table hanging in the air! A chef, a server, and an entertainer go with you to make a perfect evening. But if you're scared of heights, we don't recommend it!

The Hajime Robot Restaurant, Bangkok

Here's something *really* different – a restaurant with robots. Choose your food from a touchscreen computer menu, and a few minutes later, a smiling robot brings it to you. You can also barbecue food at your table or order other delicious Asian dishes from the menu. Try a green tea smoothie and then sit back and enjoy the entertainment – every hour the robots dance to music! It's a fun and lively atmosphere, and the service is excellent!

C Read the article again, and answer these questions. Explain your answers to a partner.

1. What can you do if you feel cold at the Chillout ice restaurant?
2. What dish does the writer recommend there?
3. How many people can dine in the sky at one time?
4. Who goes up with the guests at Dinner in the Sky?
5. What can you order at the Hajime Robot Restaurant?
6. Why do you think people try restaurants like these?

2 Listening and writing Do you recommend it?

A 3.38 Listen to Olivia talk about a restaurant she went to last week. What do you find out about it? Circle the correct words.

1. The restaurant was **Italian / Spanish**.
2. They serve great **seafood / pasta**.
3. Olivia had **a rice dish / a seafood salad**.
4. It's good for **meat eaters / vegetarians**.
5. The service was **fast / slow**.
6. The atmosphere was **fun / relaxed**.
7. It was **expensive / inexpensive**.
8. Olivia **recommends it / doesn't recommend it**.

B Read the review and the Help note. Underline the adjectives that describe the Healthy Bites restaurant.

RESTAURANT REVIEW: Healthy Bites

Last week I had dinner at a small neighborhood restaurant called Healthy Bites. It serves healthy fast food, and it is famous for its hamburgers. The food is excellent. The hamburgers come with delicious toppings like spicy cabbage with onions and a lot of garlic. The service was excellent – fast but friendly. I highly recommend it.

Help note

Useful expressions

Was it . . .	*good?*	*bad?*
The restaurant was	*good.*	*terrible.*
The service was	*excellent.*	*slow.*
The servers were	*friendly.*	*unfriendly.*
The meal was	*delicious.*	*awful.*
The food was	*tasty.*	*tasteless.*
The potatoes were	*hot.*	*cold.*

About you **C** Write a review of a restaurant you know. Talk about the atmosphere, the food, the service, and the price.

D Read your classmates' reviews. Which restaurant would you like to try?

3 Talk about it What are your favorite places to eat?

Group work Discuss the questions. Agree on a place you'd like to go to together.

- How often do you go out to eat?
- When you eat out, do you go to restaurants? cafés? fast-food places? food stands?
- Do you have a favorite place to eat? Where is it? Why do you like it?
- Where can you get good, cheap food?
- Where can you hang out with friends?
- Which restaurant in your city would you like to try?
- Which restaurant don't you recommend? Why not?

Learning tip *Grouping vocabulary*

You can group some vocabulary by the things you like and don't like.

1 Which of these types of food do you like? Which don't you like? Complete the word webs.

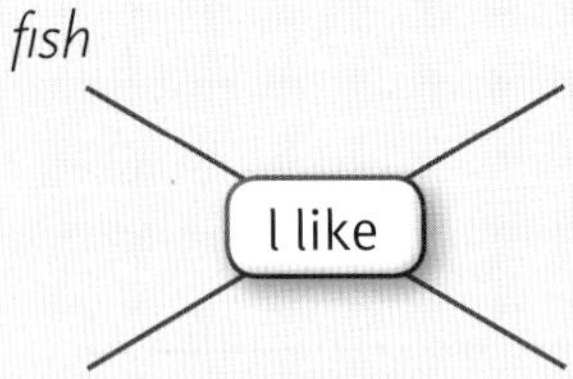

- ✓ cereal
- ✓ fish
- fruit
- meat
- milk and cheese
- pasta and bread
- shellfish
- vegetables

2 What foods do you love, and which do you hate? Complete the chart.

I love . . .	I like . . .	I don't like . . .	I can't stand . . .
			onions

In conversation

Talk about food

The top food words people use with the verb ***eat*** are:

1. meat
2. beef
3. popcorn
4. eggs
5. fish
6. steak
7. vegetables
8. seafood
9. cheese
10. cookies
11. pizza
12. bread

On your own

Label your food at home in English.
Learn the word before you eat the food!

Can Do! Now I can . . .

✓ I can . . . ? I need to review how to . . .

- ☐ talk about foods I like and my eating habits.
- ☐ make offers of food and drink.
- ☐ use *or something* and *or anything* in lists.
- ☐ end *yes-no* questions with *or . . . ?*
- ☐ understand conversations about eating habits.
- ☐ understand a conversation about a restaurant.
- ☐ read a restaurant review.
- ☐ write a restaurant review.

1 What's the question?

Complete the conversation with information questions. Then practice with a partner.

A I'm so tired this morning.
B So *what did you do last night* ?
A Last night? Oh, I went to see a band.
B You did? ________________ ?
A The Mall Kids. They're a new group.
B Yeah? ________________ ?
A They were great. I was at the club really late.
B ________________ ?
A Around 2:00 a.m. So anyway, ________________ ?
B Oh, I just went home and watched TV. The usual.
A Well, let's go out tonight or something.
B Oh, OK. ________________ ?
A Actually, I'd like to see The Mall Kids again.
B OK. But let's not stay out too late. We both have to work tomorrow!

2 Do you have a balanced diet?

A **Think about the different types of food you eat. Complete the chart.**

I eat a lot of . . .	I don't eat many . . .	I don't eat much . . .	I never eat . . .

B **Pair work Compare your chart with a partner. Ask follow-up questions.**

A I eat a lot of meat.
B Really? How much do you eat? Do you eat it every day?

3 Ask a question in two ways; answer and ask a similar question.

A **Think of a *yes-no* question to add to each question below. End the question with *or . . . ?***

1. How was your weekend? I mean, *did you do anything special or . . .* ?
2. What did you do last summer? I mean, ________________ ?
3. What did you do for your last birthday? I mean, ________________ ?
4. What would you like to do tonight? I mean, ________________ ?

B **Pair work Ask and answer the questions. After you answer a question, ask a similar one.**

A How was your weekend? I mean, did you do anything special or . . . ?
B Well, I went to the beach on Saturday. How about you? What did you do?

4 What's the right expression?

Complete the conversation with these expressions. (Use *anyway* twice.) Then practice with a partner.

or something	Good for you	anyway	Congratulations	You did
✓ or anything	good luck	I know	thank goodness	I'm sorry to hear that

Bryan How was your weekend? Did you go away *or anything* ?
Julia No, but I went to a karaoke club.
Bryan Really? ____________ ? So how was it?
Julia Great! I sang in a contest and won $50.
Bryan ____________ ! I didn't know you were a singer.
Julia Well, I practiced every day for a month.
Bryan ____________ !
Julia And ____________ I practiced! Ten of my friends were there. So, ____________ , did you do anything special?
Bryan Not really. I had to study for an exam on Saturday and Sunday. I studied all weekend and then got sick.
Julia ____________ . You need to take care of yourself.
Bryan Yeah. ____________ . . . . Well, ____________ , I have to go. I want to study my notes. But after the exam, let's meet for coffee ____________ .
Julia OK. So ____________ with your exam.

5 Show some interest!

A **Complete each sentence with a simple past verb. Then add time expressions to five sentences to make them true for you.**

1. I *went* on an interesting trip. *I went on an interesting trip last month.*
2. I ________ some new clothes.
3. I ________ someone famous.
4. I ________ an international phone call.
5. I ________ a party at my house.
6. I ________ some Italian food.
7. I ________ on the beach.
8. I ________ English with a tourist.
9. I ________ some money.
10. I ________ lost in the city.

B **Pair work** Take turns telling a partner your sentences. Respond with *You did?* and ask questions.

A I went on an interesting trip last month.
B You did? Where did you go? . . .

UNIT 1 The name game

Group work Follow the instructions below. Continue the game until you know all the names of the students in your group.

Student A: Say your full name. If you have a middle name or nickname, say it.

Student B: Repeat Student A's name. Then say your name.

Student C: Repeat the names of the other students in your group.

Then say your name.

A ***My full name is Rumiko Noguchi. I don't have a middle name or a nickname.***

B ***OK. Your name is Rumiko Noguchi. My name is Carlos Sanchez. My nickname is Flaco.***

C ***Your name is Carlos Sanchez. Your nickname is Flaco. And your name is Rumiko Noguchi . . .***

UNIT 2 What do you remember?

1 Look at the picture. Where are the things in the room? Study the picture for two minutes and try to remember.

2 **Pair work** Close your books. Make a list of the things in the room and where they are. How much can you remember? Then open your books and check.

1. chair - next to the window
2. table - in front of the chair

A ***The chair is next to the window.***

B ***Right. And the table is in front of the chair.***

UNIT 3 Guess the famous person.

Pair work Think of a famous living sports star, movie star, musician, or singer. Take turns asking your partner *yes-no* questions to guess the famous person he or she is thinking of. You can ask 10 questions!

A *Is the person female?*
B *No.*
A *Is he a sports star?*
B *Yes, he is.*
A *Is he a soccer player?...*

Useful language

Is the person male / female?
Is he / she . . . ?
- a sports star – a soccer player
- a player for (name of the team)
- an actor / a movie star
- a singer / a rock star / in a band
- a musician / a guitar player

Is he / she . . . ?
- married / single
- old / young
- an actor / a movie star
- interesting / smart / funny
- from China / from Turkey

UNIT 4 Do you have the same media habits?

Pair work Read these facts about young adults in the United States. Are you the same or different? How about your partner? Take turns asking questions. Write *S* for *Same* and *D* for *Different.*

	You	Your partner
97% of young adults use the Internet every day.		
83% use social networking sites.		
15% of young adults write blogs		
96% of young adults have a cell phone.		
66% have a smartphone.		
Young people spend only 20 minutes a day on phone calls.		
They send and receive an average of 110 text messages a day.		
They watch television two to three hours a day.		
81% use their phones and watch TV at the same time.		

A *Do you use the Internet every day?*
B *Yes, I do. I check my email every morning. How about you?*
A *Well, I check my email all day. So, yeah.*

UNIT 5

Favorite free-time activities

1 Make guesses about your partner. Write your guesses in the chart under *My guesses*.

	My guesses	My partner's answers
What does he / she usually do on weeknights?	*watches TV*	
What kinds of TV shows does he / she like?		
What's his / her favorite TV show?		
How often does he / she watch TV news?		
Does he / she sleep late on the weekends?		
What's his / her favorite weekend activity?		
How often does he / she go to the movies?		
What kinds of movies does he / she like?		
Does he / she play a sport?		
Does he / she ever go to clubs?		
Is he / she a good dancer?		
What does he / she do after class?		
What kinds of restaurants does he / she go to?		
Does he / she like shopping?		
What hobbies does he / she have?		

2 **Pair work** Take turns asking the questions in two ways to find out if your guesses were right. When you answer, use *I mean* to say something more.

A ***What do you usually do on weeknights? Do you watch TV?***

B ***Yeah, I do. I watch my favorite reality show. I mean, I don't watch TV every night. On the weekends, I go out and . . .***

Free talk

UNIT 6

Find the differences.

1 Pair work Look at the two neighborhoods below. How many differences do you see? Make a list.

Washington Circle

Lincoln Square

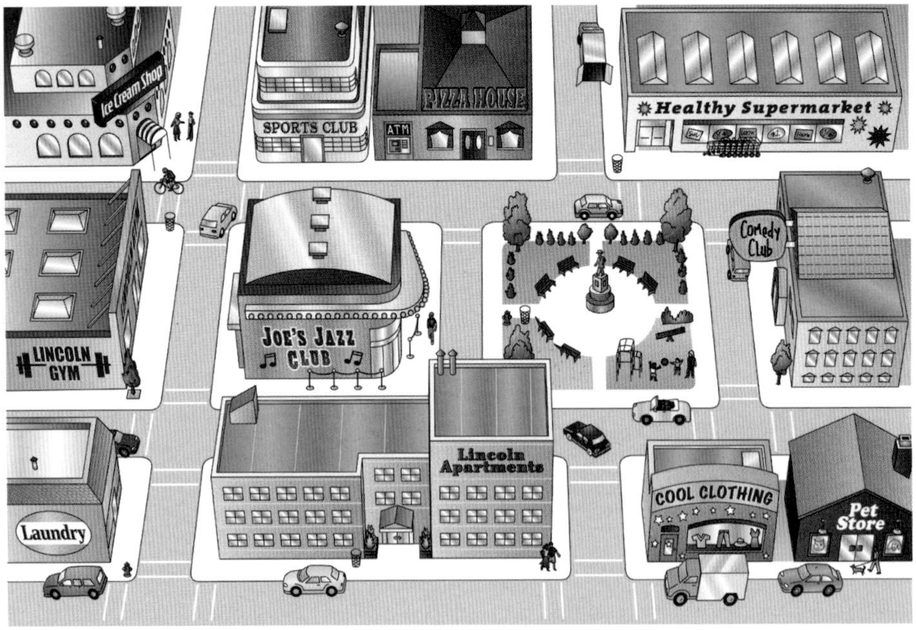

A *There's a big park in Washington Circle.*

B *There's a park in Lincoln Square, but it's very small. So that's one difference.*

Differences

1. There's a big park in Washington Circle, but there's a small park in Lincoln Square.

2 Pair work Discuss the things you like about the neighborhoods above. Are they like your neighborhood?

A *I like Washington Circle. It has a big park.*

B *Me too. There are a lot of parks in my neighborhood.*

UNIT 7 Find out about your classmates.

1 Class activity Find classmates who answer *yes* to the questions. Write their names in the chart. If someone answers *yes*, ask a follow-up question to find out more information.

Find someone who . . .	Name	More information
is taking music lessons.		
is in a band.		
is working two jobs.		
is looking for a new job.		
is eating out a lot these days.		
isn't getting enough sleep.		
is playing on a sports team.		
isn't getting enough exercise.		
is shopping for a new laptop or cell phone.		
is writing a blog.		

A ***Are you taking music lessons?***
B ***Yes, I am. I'm taking piano lessons.***
A ***That's great. How are they going?***
B ***Great. I'm learning a lot.***

2 Class activity Tell the class one interesting thing you found out about a classmate.

UNIT 8 Think fast!

Group work Think of an idea for each item below. You have two minutes! Then compare ideas with your group. Does anyone have the same answers?

Think of . . .

- a gift you have to get for someone ____________________
- something you need to buy ____________________
- a store you need to go to ____________________
- something you don't want to do, but you have to do ____________________
- a sport you want to try ____________________
- a sport you don't want to try ____________________
- something you like to wear to class ____________________
- something you need to do after class ____________________
- something you have to wear to a wedding ____________________
- a TV show you like to watch ____________________
- someone you need to call ____________________

Free talk

UNIT 9 Where in the world?

1 Pair work Where in the world can you do these things? Use the photos to help you.

Where can you . . .

1. see an amazing palace?
2. see a historic neighborhood?
3. take a cable car?
4. swim at a beautiful beach?
5. hear traditional music?
6. take a boat trip on a river?

Istanbul, Turkey

Rio de Janeiro, Brazil

Mexico City, Mexico

Merida, Venezuela

Paris, France

Tokyo, Japan

2 Pair work Choose a country you know about. Brainstorm ideas about all the interesting things you can do there. Explain any new words to your partner.

A *OK, let's make a list for Australia.*
B *Well, you can see some amazing animals, like koalas.*
A *What's a koala?*
B *Oh, it's kind of like a little bear. They're gray and white.*

UNIT 10 Yesterday

1 Look at Mario's apartment. What did he do yesterday? Study the picture for two minutes. Then close your book and make a list. How much can you remember?

2 **Pair work** Compare your lists. Did you do any of the same things as Mario? Tell your partner.

A *Did Mario do the laundry yesterday?*

B *Yes, he did. I have that on my list.* OR *I don't know. I don't have that on my list.*

A *Yeah, I did my laundry and my roommate's laundry yesterday.*

B *You did? Good for you.*

UNIT 11 Guess where I went on vacation.

1 Choose a beautiful or exciting city or country. Imagine you went there on vacation. Think of answers to these questions. Write notes in the chart.

How did you get there? Did you take a train or bus? Did you fly? Did you drive?	
How long did the trip take?	
What time of year was it?	
What was the weather like?	
What did you do there?	
What did you wear?	
What kind of food did you eat?	
What souvenirs did you buy?	
What language do they speak there?	

2 **Pair work** Ask questions like the ones above (but not "Where did you go?") to guess where each person went on vacation. How many questions do you need to guess the city or country?

A *How did you get there? Did you fly?*

B *No, I took the bus.*

A *OK. So how long did the trip take? Was it a couple of hours?*

UNIT 12 Give it a try.

1 Complete the chart. Try and write the same ideas as other classmates. Write your ideas in two minutes.

Think of something . . .	
a picky eater doesn't eat.	
tasty for breakfast.	
you have in your refrigerator that most people don't have.	
you drink a lot of.	
you would like to try for dinner.	
you don't have much of in your kitchen.	
a vegetarian would like to eat.	

2 **Group work** Compare your ideas. Score one point each time you have the same answer as a classmate. Who has the most points?

A ***Well, picky eaters don't eat much seafood or fish or anything.***

B ***That's true. I wrote vegetables.***

C ***I wrote seafood. So Miki and I both get a point because we have the same answer.***

3 **Group work** Find out your classmates' tastes. Ask about the things you wrote in the chart above.

A ***Do you eat a lot of seafood or . . . ?***

C ***No. We never have any in the house!***

Sounds right

UNIT 7

3.45 **Listen and repeat the words. Notice the underlined sounds. Are the sounds like the sound in *four* or the sound in *word*? Circle the correct word.**

1. learn (four / word)
2. morning (four / word)
3. perfect (four / word)
4. sport (four / word)
5. warm (four / word)
6. work (four / word)

UNIT 8

3.46 **Listen and repeat the words. Notice the underlined sounds. Check (✓) the sounds that are like the sound in *hat*.**

☐ 1. backpack
☐ 2. mall
☐ 3. black
☐ 4. necklace
☐ 5. bracelet
☐ 6. pants
☐ 7. briefcase
☐ 8. sale
☐ 9. cap
☐ 10. sunglasses
☐ 11. jacket
☐ 12. watch

UNIT 9

3.47 **Listen and repeat the words. Notice the underlined sounds. Are the sounds like the sound in *she* or the sound in *child*? Write *sh* or *ch*.**

1. Chile *ch*
2. French _____
3. Portuguese _____
4. Spanish _____
5. Chinese _____
6. information _____
7. question _____
8. statue _____
9. chocolate _____
10. natural _____
11. Russian _____
12. sugar _____
13. delicious _____
14. ocean _____
15. show _____
16. Turkish _____

UNIT 10

3.48 **Listen and repeat the words. Notice the underlined sounds. Are the sounds like the sounds in *looked*, *bought*, *spoke*, or *left*? Write the words from the box in the correct columns below.**

brought	cooked	met	read	saw	told
chose	drove	put	said	thought	took

looked	bought	spoke	left
	brought		

UNIT 11

3.49 **Listen and repeat the words. Notice the underlined sounds. Which sound in each group is different? Circle the odd one out.**

1. hard — part — scared — smart
2. autograph — relaxed — nervous — parasailing
3. first — nervous — snorkeling — worry
4. back — exactly — happy — vacation

UNIT 12

3.50 **Listen and repeat the words. Which syllable in each word is stronger than the other syllable(s)? Underline the stressed syllables.**

1. butter
2. pasta
3. carrot
4. pepper
5. cucumber
6. potato
7. pizza
8. sugar
9. melon
10. tomato
11. onion
12. water

UNIT 7 Lesson A Present continuous statements

A **Complete these text messages using the verbs in parentheses.**

FROM: Ava Williams **4:00 p.m.**
Hey, Olivia! I hope you __________ (not / work). The weather is so beautiful! I __________ (have) coffee with Lily at an outdoor café. We __________ (chat) about work and things. And she __________ (check) the Internet for a good movie. Are you free tonight? XXOO, Ava

FROM: Olivia Martinez **4:05 p.m.**
Ava, I'm not at work. I'm home with my parents, but we __________ (work) very hard! My mother __________ (clean) the car, and my father and I __________ (do) the laundry. I __________ (not / have) much fun! But I'm free around 5:00 p.m. Call me! –Olivia

FROM: Brandon Brown **5:00 p.m.**
Hey, John. Eric and I __________ (relax) here at the beach. Eric __________ (swim), and I __________ (send) text messages! But we __________ (get) hungry now. There's a great new restaurant near here. Let's meet for dinner. –Brandon

FROM: John Harris **5:30 p.m.**
Brandon, I'm sorry, but I __________ (stay) home this weekend. I __________ (study) for exams. Also, I __________ (write) an essay for my English class. So I __________ (not / go out) all weekend. Let's do something after my exams, OK? –John

About you **B** **Pair work** **Imagine it's Saturday evening. Write a text message to tell your partner what you're doing. Then answer your partner's message.**

UNIT 7 Lesson B Present continuous questions

Common errors

Check the spelling of verb + *-ing*.

having (NOT ~~haveing~~)
shopping (NOT ~~shoping~~)

A **Complete these phone conversations with present continuous *yes-no* and information questions. Use the words in parentheses. Compare with a partner.**

1. A Hi, it's Jeremy. How are things?
   B Pretty good. So what's up? __________ from? (where / you / call)
   A From work. I have a new job.
   B Really? __________? (where / you / work)
   A At Angelo's Pizza. You know, with Mike.
   B Oh, right. __________ tonight? (he / work)
   A No, he's not. He only works during the day.
   B OK. __________ a break right now? (you / take)
   A Yeah. I'm having pizza! I love this job! . . .

2. A Hi, it's me, Lauren. __________ at a good time? (I / call)
   B Sure. I'm just watching TV.
   A Oh. __________? (what / you / watch)
   B A rock concert on Channel 10.
   A Wow. __________? (who / sing) She has a great voice!
   B I'm not sure. But, yeah, she's amazing.

About you **B** **Pair work** **Practice the conversations. Then practice again with your own information.**

Extra practice

UNIT 8

Lesson A *Like to, want to, need to, have to*

A Use the words given to complete the questions.

1. (you / like / wear) *Do you like to wear* a different outfit every day?
2. (your family / like / go) __________________ shopping together?
3. (you and your friends / want / go) __________________ to the mall this weekend?
4. (you and your friends / like / wear) __________________ the same colors?
5. (your parents / need / buy) __________________ something new for your home? I mean, (what / they / have to / get) __________________?
6. (you / like / look around) __________________ electronics stores?
7. (Where / your best friend / like / buy) __________________ his or her clothes?

About you **B Pair work** **Ask and answer the questions. Give your own information.**

> **Common errors**
>
> Don't forget the word ***to***.
>
> *I like **to** shop online.*
>
> (NOT *I ~~like shop~~ online.*)

UNIT 8

Lesson B *How much . . . ?; this, these; that, those;* saying prices

A Look at the pictures. Complete the conversations with words from the box. You need to use some words more than once. Sometimes there is more than one answer.

it	they	this	that	these	those	is	are

1. **Clerk** Can I help you?
   Sophia Yes. This __________ a great jacket. How much is __________?
   Clerk Um, . . . __________ jacket is $199, I believe.
   Sophia And what about __________ pants? How much __________ they?
   Clerk I think __________'re $119.
   Sophia Wow. __________'re expensive! Um . . . I have to think about it. But thanks anyway.

2. **Clerk** Do you need some help?
   Austin Yeah. How much __________ those sweatshirts? There's no price tag.
   Clerk __________? They're $29.99. They're on sale.
   Austin And what about __________ sweatpants? How much are __________?
   Clerk Uh, these __________ $19.75. They're on sale, too.
   Austin OK. I want to try on a blue sweatshirt and blue sweatpants.

About you **B Pair work** **Practice the conversations with a partner. Can you think of a different ending for each conversation?**

UNIT 9

Lesson A *Can* and *can't* for possibility

A **Complete these questions and answers with *can* or *can't* and one of the verbs in the box. You can use some verbs more than once. Then practice with a partner.**

do eat buy go ride swim take walk

1. A What ___can___ you ___do___ for exercise in your neighborhood?
   B You __________ __________ a bike in the park, and you __________ __________ at the pool.
2. A What international restaurants __________ you __________ to?
   B You __________ __________ at Chinese, Korean, and Thai restaurants.
3. A __________ you __________ the latest fashions in your neighborhood?
   B Yes, you __________. There's a great store near my house.
4. A __________ people __________ around your neighborhood late at night?
   B Well, you __________ __________ a walk in the park. It's not a good idea.
5. A __________ people __________ a ferry to work in your city?
   B No, they __________. But they __________ __________ to work by subway or bus.

✕ Common errors

Use a simple verb after ***can*** and ***can't***.

*I can **take** the bus.*
(NOT *I can ~~taking~~ the bus.*)

About you **B** **Pair work** **Ask and answer the questions. Give your own answers.**

UNIT 9

Lesson B *Can* and *can't* for ability

A **Unscramble the questions. Then compare with a partner.**

1. What sports / you / play well / can ______________________________?
2. you / play / Can / a musical instrument ______________________________?
3. ride / a motorbike / you / Can ______________________________?
4. drive / can / in your family / Who ______________________________?
5. you / Can / name / all the countries in South America ______________________________?
6. music / read / you / Can ______________________________?
7. international / you / cook / any / Can / foods ______________________________?
8. speak / or understand / What languages / you / can ______________________________?

About you **B** **Pair work** **Ask and answer the questions. Give your own answers.**

Extra practice

UNIT 10 Lesson A Simple past statements: regular verbs

A Complete these statements with a past form of the verbs in parentheses.

1. It __________ (rain) yesterday, so I __________ (not / walk) home from work.
2. I __________ (not / work) late last night because I __________ (want) to go to the gym.
3. My parents __________ (not / want) to cook last night, so we __________ (order) food from a restaurant.
4. I __________ (try) to call my best friend last night, but she __________ (not / answer) her phone.
5. A classmate __________ (text) me last night, and then we __________ (chat) online.
6. I __________ (not / clean) the house on Saturday. I just __________ (relax).
7. I __________ (need) to go shopping for some new clothes on Saturday, but I __________ (not / have) time.
8. The neighbors __________ (invite) us over for dinner on Sunday. We really __________ (love) the food.

About you **B Pair work Choose five of the sentences above and make them true for you. Tell your partner.**

UNIT 10 Lesson B Simple past *yes-no* questions

A Complete these questions and answers with *did, didn't,* and the verb in parentheses. Then practice with a partner.

1. A __________ you __________ (go) shopping last weekend?
   B Yes, I __________. I __________ (buy) a new jacket.
2. A __________ you __________ (get up) early today?
   B No, I __________. I __________ (sleep) late this morning.
3. A __________ you __________ (have) a big breakfast?
   B No, I __________. I just __________ (have) coffee.
4. A __________ you __________ (spend) time on the computer last night?
   B Yes. I __________ (do) some work. I __________ (write) a report.
5. A __________ your best friend __________ (go out) with you last weekend?
   B Yes, she __________. We __________ (see) a movie together.
6. A I didn't come to class last week. __________ the teacher __________ (give) us homework?
   B No, he __________. But he __________ (give) us a test.

Common errors

In questions, don't use a simple past form after **did**.

***Did** you **go** shopping?*
(NOT ~~*Did you went*~~ *shopping?*)

About you **B Pair work Ask and answer the questions. Give your own answers.**

UNIT 11 Lesson A Simple past of *be*

A Unscramble the questions. Then complete the answers with *was, wasn't, were,* or *weren't.* Practice with a partner.

When you were little . . .

1. A strict / your / Were / parents *Were your parents strict?*
   B No, they ________ very strict with me. They ________ pretty relaxed about things.
2. A school / Was / elementary / your / big ______________________?
   B No, it ________. It ________ a small school with 50 children.
3. A in / class / your / Were / friends / your ______________________?
   B Yes, they ________. We ________ all in the same class.
4. A a good student / Were / you ______________________?
   B Well, I ________ OK. I always did my homework.
5. A nice / your / Was / teacher / first ______________________?
   B My first teacher ________ nice, but some teachers ________ very strict.
6. A you / on / Were / a sports team ______________________?
   B No, I ________ on a sports team, but I ________ a good swimmer.

About you **B Pair work** **Ask and answer the questions. Give your own information.**

UNIT 11 Lesson B Simple past information questions

A Complete the questions in the conversation. Use a question word and a verb in the simple past. Then practice the conversation with a partner.

Jim I see you're back in the office. *How was* ______________ your vacation?
Liz It was great. Really exciting.
Jim So ______________________ go?
Liz I went to Brazil. To the Amazon.
Jim Wow! ______________________ there?
Liz I was there for over a week. It was wonderful.
Jim It sounds great. So ______________________ do exactly?
Liz Well, I went on a boat trip – a nature tour. There were about 40 other people on the boat. And there was a guide. It was amazing.
Jim Nice. So ______________________ like?
Liz He was smart and very interesting. I learned a lot.
Jim And ______________________ the weather?
Liz Oh, it was hot and humid. And I mean, *very* hot!
Jim Really? So ______________________ back?
Liz Actually, I got back four days ago. I always rest for a couple of days after a vacation!

About you **B Pair work** **Think about a trip you took. Start a conversation like the one above.**

Extra practice

UNIT 12 Lesson A Countable / uncountable nouns

A Complete the questions with *much*, *many*, or *a lot of*. Sometimes there is more than one answer. Complete the answers with *a* or *an*. Write (–) if you don't need *a* or *an*.

1. A How ___*much*___ fish do you eat? Do you eat a lot?
   B Actually, I don't like ___–___ fish. I'm kind of picky.
2. A Do you eat __________ vegetables?
   B Actually, I eat __________ raw carrot every day for my mid-morning snack.
3. A How __________ fruit do you eat?
   B Well, I love __________ apples. I usually have __________ apple after dinner.
4. A Do you eat __________ red meat?
   B No, I don't. I don't like __________ red meat.
5. A How __________ cereal do you eat for breakfast?
   B I don't eat cereal. I usually have __________ egg with toast.
6. A How __________ times a week do you go out for dinner?
   B Once or twice a week. I'm a big fan of __________ Italian restaurants.

> **Common errors**
> With uncountable nouns, don't use *a / an* or add *-s*.
> *I just had some milk.*
> (NOT *I just had ~~a milk / some milks~~*.)

About you **B Pair work** Ask and answer the questions. Give your own answers.

UNIT 12 Lesson B *Would like; some* and *any*

A Unscramble the questions. Then complete the conversations with *some* or *any*. Compare with a partner.

1. A Would / some / you / coffee / like *Would you like some coffee?*
   B Sure, but we don't have ___*any*___ milk. I can get ___*some*___.
2. A you / like / Would / go out / to / for lunch ______________________?
   B Actually, I just ordered a big pizza. Would you like __________?
   A I'd love __________. I'm starving. I didn't have __________ breakfast.
3. A some / like / cookies / Would / you ______________________?
   B No, thanks. I don't want __________ right now. But can I have __________ later?
4. A tonight / to / Where / eat / would / like / you ______________________?
   B Well, there are __________ good seafood restaurants around here. I'd really like __________ fish.
5. A like / do / to / would / What / you / for your birthday ______________________?
   B I'd like to invite __________ friends over for dinner. But I don't want __________ gifts!

About you **B Pair work** Ask and answer the questions. Give your own answers.

Illustration credits

Harry Briggs: 5, 9, 14, 24, 31, 127, 129, 146 **©Cambridge University Press:** 6 *(leaf, left)*; 7 *(book, left)*; 25 *(heads)*; 54 *(building graphic, top right)*; 56 *(clocks, center)*; 100 *(calendar, background)*; 124 *(utensils, top left)* **Bunky Hurter:** 22, 32, 50, 86, 135 **Kim Johnson:** 10, 20, 30, 42, 52, 62, 74, 84, 96, 106, 116, 126 **Scott Macneil:** 54, 132 **Frank Montagna:** 12, 13, 19, 68, 79 **Q2A studio artists:** 119 **Gavin Reece:** 16, 46, 66, 120 **©Shutterstock:** 6 *(barcode, tree, airplane)*; 7 *(dumbbell, right)*; 44 *(clock, top left)*; 47 *(emoticons)*; 88 *(map)*, 92 *(map)*; 114 *(background)*; 115 *(background)* **Lucy Truman:** 6, 17, 26, 27, 34, 78, 118

Photography credits

Back cover: ©vovan/Shutterstock **8, 28, 29, 38, 39, 58, 59** ©Cambridge University Press **18, 19, 48, 49, 70, 71, 80, 81, 90, 91, 102, 103, 112, 113, 122, 123** ©Frank Veronsky **viii** *(left)* ©Design Pics/SuperStock; ©Aldo Murillo/istockphoto **1** *(clockwise from top left)* ©Don Hammond/MediaBakery; ©iofoto/Shutterstock; ©Tom Merton/MediaBakery **2** *(left)* ©Sigrid Olsson/Getty Images/RF; *(right)* ©Tetra Images/Getty Images/RF **3** *(left)* ©Photosindia/Alamy; *(right)* ©Fuse/Getty Images/RF **4** *(clockwise from left)* ©PT Images/Shutterstock; ©Monkey Business Images/Shutterstock; ©Chris Ryan/MediaBakery; ©Suprijono Suharjoto/istockphoto **6** *(left to right)* ©DV/MediaBakery; ©mangostock/Veer Images; ©Simon Greig/MediaBakery **9** *(left)* ©MediaBakery; ©Sam Edwards/MediaBakery **11** *(clockwise from top left)* ©l i g h t p o e t /Shutterstock; ©Fancy/MediaBakery; ©Rachel Frank/MediaBakery; ©Stockbroker/Alamy; ©Aleksandr Markin/Shutterstock **14** *(top row, left to right)* ©BEPictured/Shutterstock; ©nuttakit/Shutterstock; ©saginbay/Shutterstock; ©shutswis/Shutterstock; *(middle row, left to right)* ©Phant/Shutterstock; ©Julia Ivantsova/Shutterstock; ©Thinkstock; ©Anthony Berenyi/Shutterstock; *(bottom row, left to right)* ©Sergej Razvodovskij/Shutterstock; ©Hemera Technologies/Thinkstock; ©Julia Ivantsova/Shutterstock; ©ayazad/Shutterstock; ©Marc Dietrich/Shutterstock **15** *(top row, left to right)* ©Verdateo/Shutterstock; ©29september/Shutterstock; ©chaoss/Shutterstock; *(bottom row, left to right)* ©Stocksnapper/Shutterstock; ©dngood/MediaBakery; *(pens)* ©Elnur/Shutterstock; *(hand)* ©motorolka/Shutterstock **20** *(top row, left to right)* ©kate_sept2004/istockphoto; ©4kodiak/istockphoto; ©Kenneth C. Zirkel/istockphoto; ©ersinkisacik/istockphoto; ©Feng Yu/istockphoto *(bottom row, left to right)* ©Skip Odonnell/istockphoto; ©Kenneth C. Zirkel/istockphoto; ©Fancy Collection/SuperStock; ©Tobias Lauchenauer/istockphoto **21** *(clockwise from top left)* ©Lorenzo Santini/Stringer/Getty Images; ©Idealink Photography/Alamy; ©Karl Weatherly/MediaBakery; ©lev radin/Shutterstock; ©AHMAD FAIZAL YAHYA/Shutterstock; ©Kemter/istockphoto **22** *(clockwise from top left)* ©AF archive/Alamy; ©WireImage/Getty; ©Ken Durden/Shutterstock; ©Duncan Grove/Alamy **23** *(top to bottom)* ©ZUMA Press, Inc./Alamy; ©Michael Regan/Getty Images; ©Moviestore collection Ltd/Alamy; ©WireImage/Getty Images; ©DFree/Shutterstock **25** ©Slobodan Vasic/istockphoto **33** *(clockwise from top left)* ©Alejandro Rivera/istockphoto; ©zhang bo/istockphoto; ©Christopher Futcher/istockphoto; ©Helen King/Corbis; ©Rob Melnychuk/MediaBakery; ©MediaBakery **34** *(clockwise from top left)* ©Flashon Studio/Shutterstock; ©Hans Kim/Shutterstock; ©Jorg Hackemann/Shutterstock; ©Joana Lopes/Shutterstock **36** *(top row, left to right)* ©Chris Schmidt/istockphoto; ©JOSE LUIS PELAEZ/MediaBakery; ©TriggerPhoto/istockphoto *(bottom row, left to right)* ©londoneye/istockphoto; ©DrGrounds/istockphoto; ©Thinkstock **39** ©Holger Mette/istockphoto **40** ©Maartje van Caspel/istockphoto *(background)* ©J. Helgason/Shutterstock **41** ©Rouzes/istockphoto **43** *(clockwise from top left)* ©Jani Bryson/istockphoto; ©Steven Robertson/istockphoto; ©Thinkstock; ©MediaBakery **44** *(top to bottom)* ©Thinkstock; ©Thinkstock; ©Thinkstock; ©Stígur Karlsson/istockphoto **47** *(top row, left to right)* ©Cory Thoman/Shutterstock; ©Alan Diaz/AP/Corbis; ©Getty Images; ©Getty Images *(bottom row, left to right)* ©John Czenke/Shutterstock; ©CBS via Getty Images; ©Cliff Lipson/CBS via Getty Images; ©John Paul Filo/CBS via Getty Images **50** *(background)* ©URRRA/Shutterstock **51** *(left to right)* ©Neustockimages/istockphoto; ©Thinkstock **53** *(clockwise from top right)* ©Jeremy Enlow/MediaBakery; ©Getty Images; ©Medioimages/Photodisc/Thinkstock; ©Thinkstock **54** *(left to right)* ©Pressmaster/Shutterstock; ©auremar/Shutterstock; ©Andre Blais/Shutterstock **56** *(top row, left to right)* ©KtD/Shutterstock; ©Crisp/Shutterstock; ©Alex Staroseltsev/Shutterstock; ©Adam Radosavljevic/Shutterstock *(middle row, left to right)* ©Hayati Kayhan/Shutterstock; ©rdiraimo/istockphoto; ©Clayton Hansen/istockphoto; ©Jose Gil/Shutterstock *(bottom)* ©dwphotos/istockphoto **57** *(left to right)* ©Valua Vitaly/istockphoto; ©Thinkstock **60** *(clockwise from top left)* ©Patti McConville/Alamy; ©Kord/MediaBakery; ©2011 Scott Lynch/FlickrVision/Getty; ©Thinkstock **61** *(top, clockwise from top left)* ©Thinkstock; ©Andrii Gatash/istockphoto; ©Bill Varie/MediaBakery; ©Momcilo Grujic/istockphoto *(bottom)* ©Danger Jacobs/Shutterstock **62** *(phone)* © lculig/Shutterstock **63** ©Dmitriy Yakovlev/Shutterstock *(news)* ©Thinkstock **64** *(top to bottom)* ©Deklofenak/Shutterstock; ©Hill Street Studios/MediaBakery **65** *(clockwise from top left)* ©Superstock/RF; ©Sergiy Zavgorodny/istockphoto; ©Krzysztof Rafał Siekielski/istockphoto; ©AFP/Getty Images; ©VisualCommunications/istockphoto; ©Courtney Weittenhiller/istockphoto **67** ©Fotosearch/SuperStock **68** *(top row, left to right)* ©technotr/istockphoto; ©Image Source Plus/Alamy; ©ozgurcankaya/istockphoto *(middle row, left to right)* ©Bill Grove/istockphoto; ©mediaphotos/istockphoto; ©Andrew Rich/istockphoto *(bottom row, left to right)* ©Judi Ashlock/istockphoto; ©Thinkstock; ©MoniqueRodriguez/istockphoto **69** ©Design Pics/SuperStock **71** *(bottom)* ©Alan Look/Icon SMI/Newscom **72** *(top to bottom)* ©PATRICK LIN/AFP/Getty Images; ©Fabrice LEROUGE/MediaBakery *(background)* ©Shutterstock **73** *(left to right)* ©Bob Thomas/istockphoto; ©Thinkstock; ©ZUMA Wire Service/Alamy; ©DreamPictures/Getty Images/RF *(tablet computer)* ©Shutterstock **75** *(left to right)* ©Asia Images Group/Getty Images/RF; ©PhotoTalk/istockphoto; ©Holger Mette/istockphoto; ©Andrew Lever/istockphoto **76** *(left to right)* ©Izabela Habur/istockphoto; ©stocknroll/istockphoto; ©Justin Horrocks/istockphoto *(background)* ©Giuseppe Parisi/Shutterstock **78** *(top row, left to right)* ©angelo gilardelli/Shutterstock; ©FrameAngel/Shutterstock; ©Tatiana Popova/Shutterstock; ©Steve Collender/Shutterstock; ©Olena Zaskochenko/Shutterstock *(bottom row, left to right)* ©Cristian Baitg/istockphoto; ©kgfoto/istockphoto; ©Lutya/Shutterstock; ©Africa Studio/Shutterstock; ©Karkas/Shutterstock; ©nito/Shutterstock; ©Karkas/Shutterstock; ©Africa Studio/Shutterstock **81** *(red scarf)* ©kedrov/Shutterstock *(striped scarf)* ©dean bertoncelj/Shutterstock *(blue glasses)* ©Teeratas/Shutterstock; *(black glasses)* ©Africa Studio/Shutterstock *(striped socks)* ©Verkhovynets Taras/Shutterstock *(black socks)* ©shutswis/Shutterstock **82** *(left to right)* ©Maksym Bondarchuk/Shutterstock; ©Jochen Tack/Alamy **83** ©kzenon/istockphoto **85** *(clockwise from top left)* ©Prisma/SuperStock; ©Photononstop/SuperStock; ©Stock Connection/SuperStock; ©Prisma/SuperStock; ©Jon Arnold Images/SuperStock; ©Ingram Publishing/SuperStock **86** *(top to bottom)* ©Thinkstock; ©Frank van den Bergh/istockphoto; ©Jay Lazarin/istockphoto; ©Terraxplorer/istockphoto; ©Bernhard Richter/istockphoto **87** ©Arif Iqball/Alamy **88** ©Jacqueline Veissid/Getty Images/RF **89** *(top row, left to right)* ©Vinicius Tupinamba/Shutterstock; ©qingqing/Shutterstock; ©Duncan Hotston/istockphoto; ©Joe Gough/Shutterstock *(bottom row, left to right)* ©Harris Shiffman/istockphoto; ©sf_foodphoto/istockphoto; ©Piyato/Shutterstock; ©Janet Hastings/istockphoto **90** *(left to right)* ©Gregory Johnston/Shutterstock; ©Matej Michelizza/istockphoto; ©Food and Drink/SuperStock; ©Thinkstock **91** *(top)* ©Atlantide Phototravel/Corbis *(bottom, left to right)* ©Mariano Pozo/age fotostock/SuperStock; ©Stacey Gamez/istockphoto; ©Eric Tadsen/istockphoto; ©Eric Tadsen/istockphoto **92** *(clockwise from top left)* ©Robert Harding World Imagery/Alamy; ©Mordolff/istockphoto; ©fototrav/istockphoto; ©Nikada/istockphoto **93** *(top to bottom)* ©Travel Pictures Ltd/SuperStock; ©beboy/Shutterstock **97** *(clockwise from top left)* ©StockLib/istockphoto; ©Juice Images/SuperStock; ©age fotostock/SuperStock; ©Blend Images/SuperStock **98** *(clockwise from top left)* ©Darren Mower/istockphoto; ©Glow Images/SuperStock; ©AVAVA/Shutterstock; ©Blend Images/SuperStock; ©oleksa/Shutterstock; ©Elena Elisseeva/Shutterstock; ©Exactostock/SuperStock *(background)* ©Varga B. Virag/Shutterstock **100** *(top row, left to right)* ©Hill Street Studios/Blend Images/SuperStock; ©Stockbroker/SuperStock; ©Suprijono Suharjoto/istockphoto *(middle row, left to right)* ©Image Source/SuperStock; ©Image Source/SuperStock; ©Corbis/SuperStock *(bottom row, left to right)* ©Thinkstock; ©Stockbyte/Thinkstock; ©Radius/SuperStock **102** *(clockwise from top right)* ©zhang bo/istockphoto; ©Anna Bryukhanova/istockphoto; ©kali9/istockphoto Bryukhanova/istockphoto; © kali9/istockphoto **104** *(background)* ©stavklem/Shutterstock **105** *(background)* ©stavklem/Shutterstock **107** *(clockwise from top left)* ©Cusp/SuperStock; ©Leigh Schindler/istockphoto; ©Blue Jean Images/SuperStock **108** *(clockwise from top left)* ©LAWRENCE MIGDALE/Getty Images; ©eyedear/Shutterstock; ©Jupiterimages/Thinkstock; ©Kenneth Wiedemann/istockphoto *(background)* ©Africa Studio/Shutterstock **109** ©kim stillwell/istockphoto **110** ©Troels Graugaard/istockphoto **111** *(top row, left to right)* ©S. Kuelcue/Shutterstock; ©Nikki Bidgood/istockphoto; ©vilainecrevette/istockphoto *(bottom row, left to right)* ©Stockbroker/SuperStock; ©Thomas_EyeDesign/istockphoto; ©Queerstock, Inc./Alamy **114** ©Amanda Rohde/istockphoto **115** *(left to right)* ©Fancy Collection/SuperStock; ©Flirt/SuperStock **117** *(clockwise from top left)* ©oksix/Shutterstock; ©Tetra Images/SuperStock; ©FoodCollection/SuperStock; ©Maria Komar/Shutterstock; ©Robyn Mackenzie/Shutterstock; ©Exactostock/SuperStock; ©Foodfolio/Photocuisin/Photocuisine/SuperStock **120** *(spinach)* ©Hong Vo/Shutterstock; *(onions and garlic)* ©Ilja Generalov/Shutterstock; *(peppers)* ©Ruslan Kuzmenkov/Shutterstock; *(green beans)* ©Andrey Starostin/Shutterstock; *(lettuce)* ©Kasia Bialasiewicz/Shutterstock; *(tomatoes)* ©Kelvin Wong/Shutterstock; *(oil)* ©undrey/Shutterstock; *(butter)* ©TRINACRIA PHOTO/Shutterstock; *(mangoes)* ©Svetlana Kuznetsova/Shutterstock; *(melon)* ©Thinkstock; *(strawberries)* ©photastic/Shutterstock; *(apples)* ©Loskutnikov/Shutterstock; *(pineapple)* ©Valentina Proskurina/Shutterstock; *(coffee)* ©Valentyn Volkov/Shutterstock; *(sugar)* ©Food and Drink/SuperStock; *(tea)* ©Anastasios71/Shutterstock; *(potato chips)* ©Aerostato/Shutterstock; *(cereal)* ©Mikhail hoboton Popov/Shutterstock; *(peanuts)* ©Drozdowski/Shutterstock; *(cookies)* ©endeavor/Shutterstock; *(ice cream)* ©neiromobile/Shutterstock; *(lamb)* ©Gregory Gerber/Shutterstock; *(shrimp)* ©Flashon Studio/Shutterstock; *(salmon)* ©Enshpil/Shutterstock; *(hamburger meat)* ©OlegD/Shutterstock **124** *(top to bottom)* ©AFP/Getty Images; ©AP Photo/Lionel Cironneau; ©SUKREE SUKPLANG/REUTERS/Newscom **125** ©Atlantide Phototravel/Corbis *(tablet computer)* ©Shutterstock **128** *(top to bottom)* ©Ryan McVay/Thinkstock; ©Pete Saloutos/istockphoto **129** *(left to right)* ©akiyoko/istockphoto; ©Thinkstock **131** ©sturti/istockphoto **134** *(top row, left to right)* ©David Pedre/istockphoto; ©Ricardo De Mattos/istockphoto *(middle row, left to right)* ©Alija/istockphoto; ©vario images GmbH & Co.KG/Alamy *(bottom row, left to right)* ©Steve Vidler/SuperStock; ©Prisma Bildagentur AG/Alamy **135** ©Thinkstock **136** *(left to right)* ©Lisa-Blue/istockphoto; ©Alexander Raths/istockphoto

Text credits

While every effort has been made, it has not always been possible to identify the sources of all the materials used, or to trace the copyright holders. If any omissions are brought to our notice, we will be happy to include the appropriate acknowledgements on reprinting.